Dreams of Passion

The Theater of
Luigi Pirandello

Roger W. Oliver

New York · New York University Press *and* London

Copyright © 1979 by New York University

Library of Congress Cataloging in Publication Data
Oliver, Roger W   1945-
  Dreams of passion.

  (The Gotham library of the New York University Press)
  Bibliography: p.
  1. Pirandello, Luigi, 1867-1936—Criticism
and interpretation.   I. Title.
PQ4835.I7Z719   852'.9'12   79-2179
ISBN 0-8147-6157-7
ISBN 0-8147-6158-8 pbk.

Manufactured in the United States of America

Dreams of Passion

The Theater of
Luigi Pirandello

The publication of this work has
been aided by a grant from the
Andrew W. Mellon Foundation.

THE GOTHAM LIBRARY
OF THE NEW YORK UNIVERSITY PRESS

The Gotham Library is a series of original works and critical studies published in paperback primarily for student use. The Gotham hardcover edition is primarily for use by libraries and the general reader. Devoted to significant works and major authors and to literary topics of enduring importance, Gotham Library texts offer the best in literature and criticism.

Comparative and Foreign Language Literature:
Robert J. Clements, Editor
Comparative and English Language Literature:
James W. Tuttleton, Editor

For my mother and my father

Contents

	Preface	ix
	Acknowledgments	xiii
1.	*L'umorismo* and the Theater	1
2.	*That's the Way Things Are (If They Seem That Way to You)* (1917)	22
3.	*Six Characters in Search of an Author* (1921)	47
4.	*Each in His Own Way* (1924)	74
5.	*Tonight We Improvise* (1929)	96
6.	*Enrico IV* (1922)	124
7.	Conclusion	153
	Notes	157
	Index	165

Preface

In 1935, a year after he won the Nobel Prize in literature and a year before his death, Luigi Pirandello wrote the following evaluation of his critics:

> The world of international literary criticism has been crowded for a long time with numerous Pirandellos—lame, deformed, all head and no heart, gruff, insane and obscure—in whom, no matter how hard I try, I cannot recognize myself, not even in the slightest degree. [1]

Although an author may not be the best judge of those analyzing his work, Pirandello had much justification for this assessment. While the state of Pirandello criticism has improved in the last forty years, there are still widely held generalizations concerning him that are at best incomplete and at worst incorrect.

From the beginning of his career, Pirandello has been identified as an intellectual playwright, someone more interested in ideas than in people, more concerned with abstractions than with their applicability to particular situations. He satirizes this reception in some of his plays, only to have them taken as further proof of his intellectuality. His characters are often attacked for being either puppets who are manipulated for his own ends or abstractions that lack the flesh and blood of humanity. That character given the most abstract speeches in any play is usually identified as a *raisonneur* figure, created to represent the playwright's viewpoint and to expound his philosophy. In Robert Brustein's opinion, for example, Pirandello is always present in his plays, if not as a character, then as "a hovering reflective intelligence—commenting, expostulative, conceptualizing." [2]

Pirandello's plays do explore such complex issues as the multiplicity of the human personality, the relativity of truth, and the difficulty if not impossibility of establishing the dividing line between reality and its illusions. The focus, however, is usually on the interaction of these concepts with the characters who must deal with the effects such ideas have on their lives. Ideas do not exist in a vacuum for Pirandello, and any attempt to discuss his philosophy at a remove from those characters, treating them as symbols or puppets, not as people, risks grave distortion of his work.

The realization by several recent critics that suffering and a compassionate response to that suffering are central concerns in Pirandello's plays has modified but not eliminated the identification of him as a primarily metaphysical writer. The further appellation of pessimist has compounded the difficulty. Although the vision of the human condition expressed in these plays is not an especially cheerful one, it still does not merit being called "pessimistic in the extreme," as Brustein and others claim.[3] Pirandello's focus is on the problems he is dramatizing, not on his attitudes toward those problems. He is less concerned with hope or despair than with the need for people, both as individuals and in groups, to try to understand the suffering of others so that no actions will be undertaken that will increase the victim's pain.

Perhaps the main problem with previous approaches to Pirandello lies in the attempt to systematize what was not intended as a system. There is no denying that Pirandello was a playwright who incorporated abstract thought into his work. Yet the emphasis is rarely on the ideas themselves; rather, it is on the effects of these ideas on characters and the theatrical images generated to embody them. As Pirandello himself wrote:

My works are born from living images, which are the perennial source of art; but these images pass through a filter of concepts that have taken hold of me. Without doubt no work of art is ever a concept in search of expressing itself through images; on the contrary, it is an image, often one of life's most vivid images, that, nourishing itself in the travails of my spirit, assumes by itself, for the sole legitimate consistency of the work of art, a universal value.[4]

The interaction between the image and the thought it clothes can be extremely complex. The temptation to focus on the ideas alone is a strong one. Yet the attention given to the conceptual side of Pirandello's writing misjudges his originality and also undermines the very complexity of the total piece by eschewing the theatrical expression of the relationship between idea and character in favor of an examination of the ideas by themselves.

Even when Pirandello wrote a theoretical work, such as his book-length essay, *L'umorismo (On Humor),* he dealt with intensely theatrical images and processes. Although the relationship between this essay and the dramatic work has been explored previously, the emphasis has been on the ideas formulated in the essay and how these ideas are then incorporated into Pirandello's plays. *L'umorismo* does more than provide a theoretical basis for a type of drama that moves from the comic to the tragic. It presents a basic image, and then a pattern of perception and response, that stands at the center of Pirandello's dramatic art. An understanding of that basic pattern and its use, both actual and metaphoric, in five of his most characteristic plays can illuminate the total achievement of the playwright and correct the imbalance that has been created by the previous emphasis on the ideas that he has woven into that design.

The ideas presented both in *L'umorismo* and the plays are neither original nor profound. Nor need they be. As Pirandello himself argues, the artist deals primarily in images, not ideas. Pirandello's genius lies in his choice of the very medium of his expression, the theater, as the source of his basic iconography. He is certainly not the first writer to view the world theatrically in a dramatic structure.[5] By extending the metaphor of life as theater (given its most popular expression in the speech beginning "All the world's a stage...")[6] into form as well as content, however, he liberates the dramatic imagination in a significant way. By building bridges between the stage and the audience, he makes possible a series of innovations in both dramaturgy and stagecraft that have still not reached a conclusion.

The basic pattern for Pirandello's vision of the theatricalization of life has its source in *L'umorismo*. The essay does not discuss theater, or the theatricalization of life. Yet in its formulation, and more important in its images, *L'umorismo* provides the matrix and blueprint for Pirandello's artistic achievements. The aesthetic precepts of the essay become the basis for the expression of a "theatricalist" vision that begins to take shape in plays that are still superficially realistic and reaches maturity in the plays of the "theater trilogy" and *Enrico IV*. The plays can certainly stand alone; *L'umorismo*, however, provides the key to viewing these plays in a way that illuminates them and suggests exactly why Pirandello is one of the seminal figures in twentieth-century drama.

Acknowledgments

This book would not have been possible without the dedicated and inspiring assistance of Eleanor Prosser. I would also like to extend my appreciation to John Chioles, Wendell Cole, Robert Clements and James Tuttleton for their encouragement and counsel and to Despina Papazoglou of New York University Press for her patient advice. I am grateful to the Pirandello heirs for their permission to quote from his works.

During the course of preparing this work, I was most fortunate to receive a Fulbright-Hays Fellowship to pursue research on Pirandello and the Italian theater. I would like to thank the United States and Italian governments for this opportunity to live and study in Rome. Finally I must try to find words to express my gratitude to my parents for the love and understanding that has accompanied and made possible all my endeavors.

O, what a rogue and peasant slave am I!
Is it not monstrous that this player here,
But in a fiction, in a dream of passion,
Could force his soul so to his own conceit
That, from her working, all his visage wanned,
Tears in his eyes, distraction in's aspect,
A broken voice, and his whole function suiting
With forms to his conceit? And all for nothing.
For Hecuba!
What's Hecuba to him or he to Hecuba,
That he should weep for her?

Hamlet, II, iii, 556–566

1.

L'umorismo and the Theater

L'umorismo, the most complete enunciation of Pirandello's aesthetic principles, was first written in 1908 and then revised and reissued in 1920. These dates are important. They indicate that although Pirandello first published the essay before he began his playwriting career—basing its chapters on a series of lectures he delivered at the girls' school where he was teaching—he returned to the essay, revising and enlarging it, after he had written over a dozen plays. Also significant is the fact that the revision was published only a year before he wrote *Sei personaggi in cerca d'autore (Six Characters in Search of An Author)* and two years before *Enrico IV (Henry IV)*, two of his greatest plays. Thus, in the middle of his career as a dramatist, Pirandello returned to his essay on humor, an essay that is not written specifically about drama but that sheds a great deal of light on his practice as a playwright.

The essence of *L'umorismo*, a treatise that includes a linguistic, historical, and comparative analysis of the word "humor," is captured in an often quoted description of an old lady and, more important, in the humorist's response to her:

I see an old woman, with her hair dyed, greasy all over with who knows what kind of horrible concoction, awkwardly made up with rouge and dressed in youthful clothes. I begin to laugh. I become *aware* that this old woman is the *opposite* of what a respectable old woman should be. I can thus, after this first superficial encounter, stop myself at this comic impression. The comic is exactly this, an *awareness* of the *opposite*. But now, if reflection intervenes and suggests to me that this old woman probably does not experience any pleasure in dressing up this way, like a parrot, but that perhaps she suffers and does this only because she is pitifully deceiving herself that, dressed as she is, hiding her wrinkles and white hairs, she will succeed in keeping the love of a husband much younger than herself, then after realizing this I am no longer able to laugh, as I did before, because this reflection has worked on me and made me go beyond the first impression, or rather, made me look more deeply within myself. From the first awareness of the opposite I have made myself pass to this *sentiment* or *feeling of the opposite*. And this is all the difference between the comic and the humorous.[1]

This graphic image of the old woman illustrates the dual focus of Pirandello's interest and his art. He begins with a careful description of the old woman's physical appearance, then moves from the objective phenomenon of the woman to his subjective apprehension of her, defining this apprehension in two stages. The first is a purely intellectual awareness of the surface, a reaction to incongruity that yields laughter. The second is an emotional understanding that combines thought and feeling in a perception of what might lie beneath that surface. This second level causes the laughter to cease, replacing it with compassion, and perhaps even tears. It is not the old woman but the perception of her that has altered, encompassing first the comic and then the more serious potentialities of the experience.

A closer investigation of this image of the old woman can lead us to a way of approaching Pirandello as a dramatic artist. The woman is a theatrical rather than a literary creation. She does not tell us about her life and the motivations that led to her actions of dyeing her hair, using excessive makeup and dressing in clothes more suitable for a younger woman. We see only her present state and must surmise the actions that created that state, like the dyeing of the hair. The motivations for her actions must also be surmised by those who observe her, her "audience." There is no outside source to provide background information. If the audience's impression of her changes, it is only because that change has occurred in the observer's mind after further reflection on the image she presents.

Moreover, her attempt to cheat reality and the way others perceive her is a theatrical trick. The old woman has used makeup and costume, two of the basic tools of the theater, to alter her physical appearance. She is creating a role, a character different from herself. Like an actress in a third-rate provincial company, however, she has performed the job poorly. Instead of convincing her audience, she has called attention not only to herself but to her use of makeup. She has revealed her identity as role player, and she is laughed at because she has done it so self-consciously.

Once the old woman's appearance elicits the response of laughter, the emphasis shifts to the person observing her, from the actress to the audience. That audience has been amused by her bungled makeup job. On reflection, is it possible, after all, that she is aware of what she has done? She may realize the ridiculousness of her persona and yet have decided that it is worth the risk in order to keep the man she loves. She has not intended the laughter and thus has failed in at least part of her deception. The existence of a deeper reason for the old woman's actions, and the possible self-realization of her grotesque image, however, has altered the way she is perceived. She may have neither this motivation nor this insight into her position, but if her observer endows her with it, then his apprehension of her will change whether she is correctly understood or not.

The complexity of *umorismo* as defined by Pirandello is therefore rooted in its ability to extend beyond one kind of perception to another perception that challenges and modifies the first. The comic is based on the *avvertimento del contrario,* the awareness of an opposite. This awareness of a superficial incongruity involves an outside standard, the "what a respectable woman should be" of the quotation. Humor, on the other had, is *il sentimento del contrario,* the feeling or sentiment of an opposite, and involves a comparison of two personal reactions. The humorist and, by extension, the audience members who are convinced by the playwright that they should view an action or a character as humorous, are thus moving beyond the apparently comic surface to the pain that may be concealed below. As this pain is revealed, a compassionate response is elicited, even though the awareness of the initial comic reaction remains, however inappropriate it may now be. Since the feeling of the second response is built on the previous comic awareness of incongruity, that comic response remains important, not only as the catalyst of *umorismo,* but as an integral part of it.

This conflict between surface appearance and deeper realities becomes the basis for both subject matter and dramatic technique. Previous discussions of the essay have focused on the former use, providing the source of the illusion-reality dialectic identified as one of Pirandello's primary concerns. His discussion in *L'umorismo* of another related dialectic, this one between life and form, has provided another wellspring for those critics trying to define a philosophical position in the plays:

> Life is a continuous flux that we try to stop, to fix in stable and determinate forms, both inside and outside of ourselves, because we are already fixed forms, forms that move in the midst of other immobile forms and that follow the flow of life until the movement stiffens, slows down and then stops. The forms in which we try to arrest and fix in ourselves this continual flux are the concepts and ideals by which we wish to preserve, in a coherent manner, all the fictions we create for ourselves, the conditions and the state in which we try to achieve stability. But inside of us, in what we call the soul, and that is the life in us, the flux continues, undetected, running under the dams and past the limits that we impose in creating a conscience and constructing a personality. In certain tempestuous moments, under attack from this flux, all of these forms of ours collapse miserably; and even the part that does not run under the dams and outside the limits, but discovers itself to us distinctly and thus is channeled into the feelings and duties that we impose upon ourselves in the habits we have marked out, at certain moments of overflow, even these parts exceed the banks and upset everything.
>
> There are some people who have restless spirits that are almost constantly amorphous and thus scornful of ever coag-

ulating or solidifying into this or that form of personality. But even for those people who are much more tranquil, who are set into one kind of form or another, the amorphous state is still possible—the flux of life is in everything.

Although it may appear that Pirandello is positing a philosophical or even psychological system, these ideas were presented more in the hope of making his needs as an artist more clear. The conflict between the forms and concepts used to create order and the sense of freedom and change that appear essential to life is less interesting to Pirandello as an abstract dialectic than as a concrete manifestation in human behavior. Because some people like the old lady create fictions or forms in an attempt to deal with life, to alter how they are perceived and how they see the world, the artist must explore both the nature of the phenomena and their consequences. Any position of relativism, based on the suggestion that an individual's personality is multifaceted and ever changing, is then presented, not as an abstract generalization, but as a perception into human nature dramatized for an audience through characters. The impulse toward generalization comes in the mind of the audience rather than in the words of the playwright. The old woman remains a concrete theatrical image even if the response to her undergoes change and analysis.

The idea of life opposing form given here is not a particularly original one. In discussing the flux of life, Pirandello is alluding to a concept similar to the *élan vital* of Henri Bergson and the life force of Friedrich Nietzsche and later George Bernard Shaw. In fact, most of the concepts in Pirandello's *L'umorismo* and plays were not original. The work of Sigmund Freud had revealed the multidimensionality of the personality, as well as the unconscious, while the formulations of Albert Einstein were defining relativity. Georg W. F. Hegel's "levels of consciousness" also can be found in the matrix of ideas from which Pirandello drew. It is in his transformation of these thoughts from the level of theory to that of artistic creation that Pirandello demonstrates his originality.

The difficulty of perception and the need for the complexity of humoristic vision can perhaps best be illustrated through Pirandello himself. In 1921 and 1923, respectively, an Italian critic, Adriano Tilgher, published two collections of essays, *Voci del tèmpo*

(Voices of the Time) and *Studi sul teatro contemporáneo (Studies in Contemporary Theater)*,[2] where he lavishly praised Pirandello and used the life-form dichotomy of *L'umorismo* to explicate the plays. Pirandello, the victim of outrageous critical and public reaction, expressed his gratitude to Tilgher for clarifying his work but was perhaps overanxious to be appreciated. What had been posited by Pirandello as one part of an approach to life was now adopted as the way of interpreting his dramatic work.

Tilgher's identification of a philosophical pattern to be found in Pirandello's work gave the playwright a prestige he had not previously achieved. It also provided an easy answer to the frequently posed question of what his plays were about. The Tilgherian dichotomy, however, limited not only the way critics would look at his past work but the shape of future work as well. The life-form conflict actually became the subject matter of some of Pirandello's later plays, such as *Diana e la Tuda (Diana and the Tuda)* and *Quando si è qualcuno* (When Someone Is Somebody), but they lack the richness and the complexity of the earlier work, in which the life-form concept was just a part of the background material out of which the central actions of the plays emerge.

In his exhaustive biographical-critical study, *Pirandello*, Gaspar Giudice argues that the playwright never equaled his achievements of *Six Characters* and *Enrico IV* because the Tilgherian dichotomy brought him a rigidity and a schema that were detrimental to his work. Giudice also asserts that Pirandello never mastered the philosophical jargon used by Tilgher and that his plays became ideological when he used the formula. Pirandello used the life-form pattern not only in his plays but in discussions of American family life, love, and Italian politics. When he finally came out publicly for Benito Mussolini, his reasons were couched in the life-form language. He claimed that the old political system was too rigid and that Mussolini represented the Italian surge of life that would bring new freedom to the country.[3]

Whereas modern critics and directors are now challenging the Tilgherian dialectic as the best way to approach Pirandello, even though the playwright espoused it and allowed it to dominate, if not destroy, his later plays, there was also contemporary disapproval of Tilgher's influence. One newspaper had Pirandello saying, "But am I me or am I Tilgher." Another asked which came first—Tilgher (the egg) or Pirandello (the chicken).[4] It is natural that antagonistic critics would mock his chief defender. It is deeply ironic that the man who strongly objected to an overly intellectual approach to his work ("lame, deformed, all head and no heart, gruff, insane and obscure") embraced the critic who most strongly fostered such an interpretation. Life imitated art, as a critical "form" was superimposed on the "life" of Pirandello's creations. Furthermore, the essay that contains the seeds of a reading that can rescue the plays from excessive abstraction served to generate their most rigid systematization, a system that was even welcomed by the author it ultimately confined.

Another interpreter, the Italian director Luigi Squarzina, artistic director of the Teatro Stábile di Roma, vigorously challenges the Tilgherian dichotomy. For Squarzina, the key lies in Pirandello's presentation of a series of changing perspectives, making him "one of the first European writers to contribute to the fragmentation of traditional structures."[5] As Squarzina sees it, this fragmentation goes far beyond Tilgher's life-form dialectic, as the following statement concerning his production of *Ciascuno a suo modo (Each in His Own Way)* makes clear:

> By moving continuously from identification to alienation and back to identification again, we presented Pirandello's reality as a playing with mirrors, as I think Pirandello really wanted it to be, but never as a Manichean dichotomy of reality—like A and B, black and white—never.[6]

Although the life-form dichotomy can sometimes be used to describe the conflict between emotion and intellect that Pirandello often explores, as well as the conflict between a role and the person underneath, Squarzina is correct in arguing that the play's complexity surpasses the simplicity of Tilgher's formulation. His insistence on dealing with the attempt of forms to organize the life spirit—a spirit that tries to assert its freedom by breaking through those formal restrictions—also places excessive emphasis on the theoretical substratum of the plays, an emphasis that overlooks the theatrical images and relationships that are of primary importance.

When Squarzina writes of mirrors in connection with Pirandello's plays, he refers to an image that is ultimately much more important to an understanding of Pirandello's dramaturgy than the life-form dialectic. Pirandello himself defined the mirror as the principle of his theater aesthetic in the following terms:

> When a man lives, he lives and does not see himself. Well, put a mirror before him and make him see himself in the act of living, under the sway of his passions: either he remains astonished and dumbfounded at his own appearance, or else he turns away his eyes so as not to see himself, or else in disgust he spits at his image, or again clinches his fist to break it; and if he had been weeping, he can weep no more; if he had been laughing, he can laugh no more, and so on. In a word, there arises a crisis, and that crisis is my theater.[7]

Actually, there are two crises in the *teatro dello spècchio* (theater of the mirror): one onstage and one in the auditorium. They are both crises of perception, however, and it is the relationship between the two, explored with great care, that establishes both Pirandello's dramaturgy and his vision of life as well. For Pirandello is ultimately much more concerned with perception than with metaphysics. The conflict between forms and a life force coursing underneath is subsidiary to the conflict between how the individual perceives the world and how others apprehend the same phenomenon.

The first crisis, involving the characters onstage, occurs when they are forced to confront something they have attempted to avoid looking at in the past and are forced to move from one level of perception to another. This confrontation may be beneficial, even though painful, or it may be disastrous, destroying an illusion that is necessary for the continuation of life. Pirandello is not an ideologue. He is not advocating the destruction of all forms, of all fictions, of all illusions. In fact, his sharpest criticism is reserved for those characters who insist on interfering with the private affairs of others, despite the possible harm they might cause. Thus, the exposure to Delia Moreno and Michele Rocca, two of the central characters of *Each in His Own Way*, that their mutual hatred is really a mask covering their love, is a necessary crisis, while the agony to which the group of gossips subjects the newly arrived

Ponza-Frola family in *Così è (se vi pare)* (*That's the Way Things Are— If They Seem that Way to You*) [8] is not.

The second kind of crisis is focused on the audience, when the playwright as humorist tries to get the spectators to make the same leap from the *avvertimento* to the *sentimento* level. The play has been a mirror of a particular aspect of life. Yet the audience's response should not stop with an examination of the characters, even if that examination probes beneath the dramatic surface to the reality of the stage life, making the connection between the ideas and emotions of the characters. The mirror in which other people's lives were reflected should now reflect something of the audience's own life. Through the crisis precipitated on stage another crisis should be caused in the spectator. If he identified with a character who was deceiving himself or wrongfully seeking information that was of no concern to him, then the revelation offered by the play can be personalized by the playgoer. Just as characters should have been presented with images that will penetrate through the intellectual conceits constituting the surface of their reality, so the audience should react in the same way. Once those characters have left the stage, the mirror reflects back to the audience images of themselves, as they confront their relationship with what they have just seen, as well as the reality of their own lives.

Sometimes Pirandello creates certain expectations in his audience by trapping them into identifying with characters who are searching for the wrong information or are engaged in dangerous pursuits. When those characters are frustrated, so is the audience. If Pirandello has functioned as a true humorist, however, the spectator's initial anger and frustration will not be his final reaction to the play. A member of the audience expecting to be told "the truth" about the family relationship between Signor and Signora Ponza and Signora Frola in *That's the Way Things Are* may, upon reflection, feel an empathy with the family's sorrow, leading to a realization that such information is certainly not the focal point of the play. A reversal will occur that will be the essence of humor. As Pirandello writes in *L'umorismo:*

> Every sentiment, every thought, every impulse that springs up in the humorist immediately splits itself into its opposite: every yes also becomes a no that in the end comes to assume

the same value as the yes. Perhaps the humorist may pretend sometimes to hold only one position: inside of him, however, the other sentiment that at first doesn't seem to have the courage to reveal itself speaks to him; it speaks to him and begins to move him; now with a timid excuse, then with a shrewd reflection that deflates the seriousness of the situation and leads to laughter.

The serious may lead to the comic, the comic to the serious. Life, particularly as seen by an Italian, is tremendously volatile. Pirandello's plays thus suggest the constant possibility of reversal both in their subject matter and in the dramatic technique employed to communicate this insight to an audience.

The humorist must be able to have the dual vision described above. One of the keys to this vision is his ability to penetrate through the surface aspects of a given reality:

> He sees the world, if not completely naked, then in its undershirt, so to speak. He sees the king, who had made such a beautiful impression when seen on the majesty of his throne, with his scepter and crown and mantle of purple and ermine, in his undershirt. Don't arrange the dead, in their shining rooms, on their catafalques, with too much pomp, because the humorist can be disrespectful of even this composition, all this apparatus; and can, for example, in the middle of the bystanders' seriousness, catch in that corpse there, cold and hard, but dressed in tails with the king's decorations, a lugubrious grumbling in the stomach, and exclaim (since such things are certainly said better in Latin): *Digestio post mortem.*

Clothes and other such realistic surface trappings fascinate the humorist because they serve as theatrically manufactured contrasts to what is being concealed underneath. The humorist can never be content to describe, since the very function of his art is to penetrate beneath the often described surface to the reality underneath that has been ignored or forgotten.

The example of the dead king presents the opposite process from that employed with the incongruously dressed and made up old woman. With her, the humorist moved from the comic to the serious. Here the surface details of the death of a monarch suggest a solemnity that is then punctured by the humorist's ability to discover the possibility of the opposite reality anywhere. The comic and tragic are never far apart when the humorist is present. It becomes his job to communicate his vision to an audience, by pointing out the grumbling that undercuts the splendor of the exquisitely appointed king. The humorist looks at life through the bifocal lens of comedy and tragedy, appreciating the fact that almost all people and their actions can be comic and sad, or at least contain their possibility, at the same time. He communicates this perception through such images as the old woman and the king and also by structuring his plays in such a way that the surface and the underlying reality are inevitably in conflict. Thus, if at first glance, Pirandello's plays may seem to be about philosophy, that is probably the last place to locate their essence.

In dramatizing his insights on the stage, Pirandello's technique as a humorist differs from the one often employed by other literary and dramatic artists. Instead of trying to create a character and make him coherent through the cumulative revelation of information, adding more and more details until a portrait is completed, he creates a superficial image of that character and then tries to break it down. In Pirandello's works, first impressions are almost always contradicted later. The appearance expressed by an accumulation of surface detail must be penetrated, since the reality covered by that detail may be the opposite of what is first seen.

In this same way Pirandello's plays begin with the dominant theatrical convention of his day, that of psychological realism. A drawing room, a salon in a villa, eventually the theater stage itself becomes the location of his drama. Yet the vision dramatized is not that of familiar reality but of life unmasked by the humorist and then reflected back to an audience in a mirror showing an altered image. This new vision, attempting to engender in the audience the "sentiment of the contrary," may thus contradict the old, comfortable representation it is used to seeing, just as Pirandello's dramaturgy seems at first to be "realistic" and then fragments into something seen from new and different perspectives.

The surface appearance the humorist must penetrate is often, in Pirandello's plays, a conscious construct intended to deceive or distract. To define the process whereby characters—and, by extension, the theatergoers whose reality they mirror—try to make themselves into something that will pass as a coherent and consistent personality, he uses the term *costruirsi (to build oneself up)*. The key to the process of *costruirsi* is the desire to create a persona, an image, that will cover over those very incongruities that the humorist seeks to expose. An appearance of unity is created to cover the reality of multiplicity. A character tries to hide the inconsistencies of his personality behind an image, a persona that will project the part of himself he wants to be seen, the part that he has built up.

The word used most often to describe these personae is "masks," and indeed the title chosen for Pirandello's total collection of dramatic work is *Maschere nude (Naked Masks)*.[9] There are many ways in which characters (and the people they reflect) can use these masks. A mask can be a fiction created as part of a *costruzióne*, of which the person using it is constantly aware. It can also be a fiction that comes to be believed in by the individual as his true reality. A mask can also be a construct that is forced upon the person by society in order to protect itself, especially if that person's behavior threatens to endanger the established order.

Pirandello does not take one consistent attitude toward the masks employed by his characters. The mask can be a protective as well as a destructive mechanism for both the individual and society. It is the humorist's job, with his mirror and the crisis it causes, to bring new insight when all perspective on the use of the mask has been lost, either by those who are wearing it or, as in the case of the group of gossips in *That's the Way Things Are*, those who capriciously try to tear it off without anticipating the possible consequences.

The very terms that Pirandello uses to express his vision of life suggest the close ties between that vision and the medium of the theater he has chosen to express it. Not only are the examples of the old woman and the dead king heavily reliant on the theatrical techniques of costume and makeup, but, the key terms of *L'umorismo*—especially *maschera* (mask), *spècchio* (mirror), and *costruirsi*—are all close to the basic act of theater as a reenactment of life. Pirandello even uses these words as an integral part of his drama, with the characters actually referring to masks and mirrors. By structuring the characters' relationships with each other through these devices, Pirandello attempts to present his audience with a vision of itself that will generate awareness of the presence of these "theatrical" devices in nontheatrical circumstances; that is, in everyday life.

The mask is one of the key ways in which Pirandello establishes the relationship between theater and life that becomes the essence of his dramaturgy. Although he suggests in his second version of *Six Characters* that the use of special masks for the characters might be the best way to distinguish them from the actors of the company, the mask is usually a metaphorical construct in his plays. From the beginnings of drama, the actor has often used a mask to help him make the transition from himself into another figure, the character he wants to be perceived as on stage. While the Greek theater and the commedia dell' arte used actual masks, even when the mask itself is not employed, the basic metaphor remains the same. Costume and makeup are then used for the same purposes, as in the Elizabethan theater, where boys could play the parts of women with the help of a metaphoric "mask."

The idea of the theatrical role as a mask is often heightened by the use of disguises that serve as masks in the plays. Here a third level of existence is created, with the actor creating a character who is trying to create another version of that character for at least some of the other characters of the play (his or her "audience"). Either in its actual or metaphoric use, then, the basic purpose of the mask as a theater device becomes the hiding of what is behind it and the projection of its image as the true one of its wearer, to be perceived as the wearer's "reality."

Pirandello's use of the metaphor of the mask allows him to make a firm connection between the mimetic art of the theater and the reality it reflects. His plays become an exploration of role playing, both on and off the stage. Whether the actor uses the physical mask or not, each role he assumes is a mask he places between the audience and himself. This idea is explored most directly in a late play, *Trovarsi (To Find Oneself)*, which presents the dilemma of a celebrated actress who has no life of her own, who lives only through her roles onstage. She tries to have a love affair, to create a life for herself outside the theater, but she discovers that she is unable to do so, that she must seek shelter in someone else's lines whenever she confronts a problem. At the play's conclusion she decides to leave the lover and return to the stage, since it is there, and only there, that she can find herself and exert any control over her life.

The metaphor of the mask as a theatrical role suggests how the theater serves as mirror of reality, as re-creator of life's actions and people. It also predicates the opposite insight, that life itself is intensely theatrical, with individuals adopting masks in order to perform roles that will create an illusion for others and even for themselves. If theater is the illusion of reality, then very often so is life itself. Theater reflects life, and life theater, with both using roles, masks, makeup, and costumes to create the perception of another reality. The theater of the mirror thus becomes mutually reflective, with each mirror pointed at the other, so that at times there is great confusion over which is originating and which is reflecting, a confusion that is at the center of Pirandello's art.

If the actor's presentation of a character can be compared to the assumption of a mask, then it can also be linked to Pirandello's concept of the process of *costruirsi.* I do not think it is purely coincidental that the Russian actor Konstantin Stanislavski entitled one of his books *Building a Character,* for the whole process of the creation of a character is an act of construction. The actor begins with the foundation of the playwright's words and ideas; he then uses his imagination, intelligence, and physical skill to build up his vision of that character. Just as a person does not construct his character in a vacuum, so the actor must take into consideration what his fellow actors are doing and how his individual work fits into the overall design of the play as conceived by playwright and director.

Pirandello's self-proclaimed role as humorist makes the choice of his theatrical technique almost inevitable. As a humorist he often strips his characters of their illusions, their *costruzióne,* so that they must face the reality of their existence. In the same way he approaches the theatrical process—the relationship between audience and presentation—and strips away some of the illusion. In certain plays actors are called actors, and the stage is acknowledged in its true identity. Since Pirandello has written a play, there is still some illusion involved, but there is also more acknowledgment of the reality of the audience's presence in a theater than had been customary in the plays written previously.

The humoristic process of moving from *avvertimento* to *sentimento,* as well as the image of the mask and the process of *costruirsi*, are often implied rather than actual metaphors in Pirandello's plays. The crucial image of the mirror, however, appears as a physical part of the stage setting as well as the metaphoric embodiment of his theater. Lamberto Laudisi, the man who challenges the attempts of his relatives and their friends to pry into the affairs of the newly arrived family in *That's the Way Things Are*, confronts his own image in a mirror, asking it which image is real and which the shadow. The climax in the use of mirrors probably occurs in *Each in His Own Way*, where physical mirrors are used to reflect images and at the same time to suggest the various levels of the play; the actors and the characters they play, the "real" people on whom the characters are based, and the "stage" and "real" audiences reflect and distort each other, illuminating the ever shifting focus of the play.

Even here the metaphoric use of the mirror image is more important than the literal one. With its presentation of real people through actions that are similar to those performed offstage (whether the play is realistic or not), the theater is the art form that most closely mirrors life by reflecting to an audience the most recognizable image of themselves. Whereas parallels between *Enrico IV* and *Hamlet* have been pointed out by several critics,[10] certain aspects of Pirandello's dramatic work as a whole can be said to have an affinity to aspects of Shakespeare's plays. Hamlet's reference to art holding a mirror up to nature comes most quickly to mind, since Pirandello himself labeled his theater a "teatro dello spècchio," a reflection of the world through the art of his theater.

It is in Hamlet's use of the visiting players, however, that a more significant connection can be made between *Hamlet* and the Italian playwright's dramaturgy. In using the players to present a play that mirrors the actions of which he suspects Claudius guilty, Hamlet hopes to spark a recognition in his uncle that will precipitate a crisis, a crisis that will supply him with the proof that Claudius in fact murdered his father. This is the same kind of crisis of recognition posited in the statement on mirrors. For Hamlet the play is "the thing/ Wherein I'll catch the conscience of the king." Although Pirandello distrusts the "conscience" as another construct of man's reason that can be as deceived, or as deceptive, as the mask, he wants to use his play in the same way Hamlet did: to force a crisis of recognition that will cause an evaluation of one's actions and perhaps an alteration in that behavior. Pirandello first uses his mirrors to catch the consciences of some of his characters and then turns them outward in his attempt to induce his audience to undergo the same kind of confrontation and recognition.

Shakespeare's use of the play-within-a-play device and Hamlet's speech to the players on acting serve as reminders that the self-conscious use of the theater to comment on itself is part of dramatic tradition. The significant originality of Pirandello's practice of what might be called theatricalism lies in the variety of ways he demonstrates this relationship between theater and life and in his ability to make this theatricalism more than mere self-conscious fascination with his medium. For Hamlet the play is a means to an end, a device to catch Claudius that is put aside as soon as it has served its purpose. Pirandello's examination of the theatrical event and its component parts is extended and reshaped into many forms because it is his end as well as his means. Since the mirror of the theater not only reflects life but also contributes to some of its basic activities, an understanding of the working of the theater is necessary for an appreciation of how and why life outside the theater is influenced by it.

Pirandello's self-conscious use of his medium also firmly places him within the realm of the Modernist approach to artistic creation. As defined by Clement Greenberg in his important essay "Modernist Painting,"[11] the distinguishing characteristic of the Modern in art is the artist's acknowledgment that he is working in his own medium. Instead of denying or camouflaging the materials at his disposal, he accepts and even emphasizes them. As Greenberg writes. "The essence of Modernism lies, as I see it, in the use of the characteristic methods of a discipline to criticize the discipline itself—not in order to subvert it, but to entrench it more firmly in its area of competence."[12]

Since Greenberg's essay concentrates on the visual arts, he discusses how the Cubists' decision to emphasize the two-dimensionality of their canvases by stressing flatness rather than perspective brings about Modernity in painting. The visual rather than the literary aspect of the painting is stressed; color, form, and texture become of prime significance, and subject matter recedes into the background. Realistic representation is secondary to the exploration of those qualities specifically characteristic of the visual experience.

Painting is obviously not the only art form that has moved away from realistic re-creation. In fact, Greenberg identifies Immanuel Kant, in using logic to establish the limits of logic and criticize the means itself of criticism, as the first true Modernist. Atonality in music, the stream-of-consciousness technique in the novel, the purity of movement to music as practiced in the choreography of George Balanchine: all participate in the same process. Formalism in any medium is a move in this direction.

In the theater, the first step toward the Modernism discussed by Greenberg is the acknowledgment of the theater stage as the location of the play's action. Although later playwrights like Samuel Beckett, Eugène Ionesco, and Jean Genet go further in presenting more subtle exploration of what Peter Brook calls "the empty space" of the theater, it is Pirandello, with his raised curtain and empty stage greeting the incoming audience of *Six Characters in Search of an Author,* who really heralds the arrival of Modernism in the theater. Although it is true that Bertolt Brecht soon experimented in a similar way with his "alienation technique," distancing both actor and audience from the realistic illusion of the play, it is Pirandello's theatricalism, despite its retention of certain illusory practices, that forged the bonds between the two sides of the footlights and made the Modernist theater possible.

Inherent, then, in Pirandello's use of the theatrical concepts of the mask and of "building oneself up" is the assumption that many of the "fictions" in which men choose to clothe themselves are theatrical illusions. Of course the mirror he is using to communicate this insight is also an illusion, with actors pretending to be people other than themselves. The humorist, as the man who penetrates through the mask and the *costruirsi* process to see the character naked, or at least in his undershirt, thus has a very important relationship to these illusions. In fact, it is this relationship that clarifies the distinction between the humorist and the writers of comedy and satire and also suggests the technique Pirandello will use as the basis of his theater:

> Let's begin with the thing that illusion makes for each of us, with the construction that each person makes for himself

through the work of illusion. Do we see ourselves in our true and genuine reality, as we are, or rather as we would like to be? Through a spontaneous artifice created from within, the fruit of secret tendencies or unconscious imitation, don't we believe ourselves, in good faith, to be what we substantially are not? And we think, work and live according to this fictitious but sincere interpretation of ourselves.

Now, through reflection, the comic and satiric writers can discover this illusory construction as well as the humorist can. But the comic writer will only laugh, content to deflate this metaphor of ourselves imposed by spontaneous illusion. The satirist will be outraged. But not the humorist; he will see through the ridiculous aspect of the discovery to the serious and dolorous side. He will take the illusory construction apart, but not solely to laugh at it, and instead of scorning it, he will feel compassion for it, while he is also laughing.

The comic and satiric writers know how much drivel the spider of experience takes from social life in order to spin the web of mentality in this individual or that; and how what we call the moral sense often remains entangled in this web. What are, fundamentally, the social relationships of so-called convenience? Calculated considerations where morality is almost always sacrificed. The humorist goes deeper, and laughs with scorn when he discoveres how, even in ignorance, with the best possible faith, we are induced to interpret, through a spontaneous fiction, as a real moral sentiment what in reality is nothing other than a consideration or feeling of convenience, that is, calculation. And he goes even deeper to discover that even the need to appear worse than we really are can become conventional, if we belong to a social group that expresses ideals and sentiments that are appropriate to the group, but which nevertheless appear contrary and inferior to our own private feelings.[13]

The humoristic artist, in whatever medium, goes beyond the comic and/or satiric perception of illusions. He tries to penetrate beneath the surface of these illusions in order to understand them in all their complexity. Most important, the humorist wants to see how and why these illusions come to be. It is this very search for complexity, and the understanding of this complexity, that produces the compassion that sets his work apart from the comic and satiric writers. Pirandello wants to undress his characters, not to laugh at or scorn them, but to come to terms with the "real" person, in all of his or her humanity. When this real person is seen, the combination of laughter and tears is the appropriate response. *Umorismo* is thus especially necessary in the twentieth century, where the human condition is perceived as an end in itself rather than as part of a larger process in which actions might be given meaning or justification by reference to some religious or cosmic process.

The theater becomes the best way of communicating this humoristic vision to others precisely because it presents the body as well as the soul of its characters. A first impression can be created by the visual appearance of a character in a certain milieu, an impression that can be contradicted by what the character later reveals through actions and the response of others. Since one illusion—that of actor as character, of stage setting as real place—is already being created, the atmosphere for the exploration of these and other illusions has been established. The connection between the illusion of the theater and the illusions of everyday life can be made without much preparation, because the art of acting, the creation of a role, a "mask," is so close to the vision of life suggested in the essay.

In the final paragraph of the passage from *L'umorismo* cited above, Pirandello stresses the importance of social relationships to the exploration of illusions. Certain activities are both determined and then granted acceptance by the pressures of societal convention. The behavior of the individual is thus strongly influenced by the attitudes of people acting together as part of a group. What better way is there to communicate this idea and to investigate its ramifications than in a theater, where individuals have come together to form a group that partakes of a common experience? It is no accident that Pirandello's plays often center on the conflict between a group of people and one or two individuals. Social pressures contribute both to the creation and destruction of illusions; and in Pirandello's complex vision, both of these acts can be beneficial and destructive, depending on the specific circumstances. Furthermore, the willingness to accept at face value the authenticity of surface appearances as apprehended by members of that group becomes intensified when shared as a group, with individual identities becoming submerged in the larger interest. And finally all of this is being perceived by individuals as part of another group: the audience.

Pirandello further merges his aesthetic, as formulated in *L'umorismo,* and his dramatic practice by structuring his plays in such a way that if the audience members do not follow his clues and perceive humoristically, they will miss the very point he is making. Those theatergoers, including critics, who stop at the intellectual aspects of Pirandello's plays, fail to penetrate the surface of his work. Humanity may try to live rationally, under the rule of logic, but when a person is in "the act of living," he or she often acts under the sway of passion. Many of the so-called philosophical speeches in Pirandello's plays, particularly those of the Father in *Six Characters,* are in reality deeply felt attempts to justify actions that were prompted by the dominance of emotion over intellect. Pirandello is investigating human nature as a complete organism, an organism that has both emotional-sentimental and rational-intellectual sides, and he accomplishes this by engaging his audience on both of these levels. These two sides often come into conflict with each other, and out of this crisis, referred to as *il sentimento del contrario,* comes the core of the theatrical work under discussion here.

Pirandello's theater, a mirror that attempts to penetrate through the facades built by people in order to reflect the reality of their inner being, does not present an exact replica of that image. It distorts, transforms, and selects. Ideas are exaggerated into bloodless abstractions, emotions into melodrama. In exploring the primal conflict between the two sides of human nature, Pirandello, as artist, emphasizes the extremities of the duality. There is also a cumulative effect. If the intellect has dominated, then emotional pressures build until they finally erupt with great force. The enormity of the passionate outburst may then require sophisticated intellectualization in order to supply the self-justification necessary to maintain the vision of self necessary for survival.

Pirandello is really too complex a playwright to settle for delivering a message in his work. Yet if one can be conjectured, it is less concerned with the ideas of the plays—illusion versus reality, the difficulty of establishing one truth, one personality, or one vision of life—than with the process of perception that is at the basis of his dramaturgy. The humorist does not stop at surface appearances— at what may first seem to be—but continues to look, to examine, to be open to feelings as well as thought. In doing this he often reverses his first perception, exchanging it for a deeper insight, one that combines both sides of human nature and that often results in a compassion missing from the initial response. Pirandello chooses a dramatic technique that challenges the validity of first impressions by an interpenetration of theater and life, his mirror and what it reflects. In creating a self-conscious, Modernist theater, he is paradoxically creating an art that penetrates into the truth of life, where the practices and ideas of the theater have become more and more central to human relationships. Pirandello's art ultimately merges subject matter and form, so that they, like thought and emotion, theater and life, and the comic and tragic response, interpenetrate to comment on and enrich each other, creating the complexity that is both Pirandello's intention and his achievement.

2.

That's the Way Things Are (If They Seem That Way to You) (1917)

When Pirandello began his career as a playwright, the dominant traditions of the Italian stage were bourgeois sentimental comedy, naturalistic social drama and the florid romaticism of Gabriele D'Annunzio.[1] While Pirandello ultimately rejected these models as the proper means of expression for his artistic vision, he did not break abruptly with the past, like the more radical experiments of Futurism, Surrealism, and Dadaism. Novelty for its own sake was of no interest to him. Instead he began with the old forms and the ways people were accustomed to viewing the world. In the presentation of a new approach to life, reality, and character, the theatrical mirror was altered to keep pace with the changes in perception being dramatized. Pirandello thus became an artistic innovator out of necessity, and his innovations succeed precisely because they grow out of the old ways of looking at both life and theater, yet at the same time reflect the alternative vision being formulated.

After having established his literary reputation as a novelist and short-story writer, Pirandello turned to the theater. At first in the one-act form, and later in full-length works, he explored the milieu and characters of his birthplace, Sicily, following in the tradition of Italian realism, known in Italy as *verismo*. This tradition had reached its culmination in the fiction and then the theater of his fellow Sicilian Giovanni Verga, whose influence can be seen both in Pirandello's fiction and in his early dramatic work. Pirandello also followed Verga's example in choosing his own short stories as material for the stage. According to Eric Bentley, "of Pirandello's forty-four plays, only ten are completely independent of his stories and twenty-eight might correctly be described as adaptations."[2]

Even when following in the footsteps of a master, Pirandello added his distinctive viewpoint. The unrelieved tragedy of the lives of Verga's peasants became tempered by the earthy humor that was also part of Sicilian life. While some of the one acts, like *La giara (The Jar)* and *Cecè*, could almost be considered farces, the full-length *Liolà*, the final and also best play of Pirandello's Sicilian period, expresses his vision most clearly. Although there is an underlying desperation in some of the characters in the play, the energy and charismatic charm of the central figure, the carefree lover Liolà, suffuse the entire play with a sense of liberation and a vitality that becomes its main dramatic impulses.

By 1917, however, the Sicilian dialect theater in which Pirandello had been working up to this time became too limiting. He wanted to express more universal concerns and did not want to use either the dialect or, more important, the stylistic restrictions of *verismo*.[3] The first attempt to write in another vein was *Così é (se vi pare)* *(That's the Way Things Are–If They Seem That Way to You)* which Pirandello based on a short story entitled "Signora Frola and Signor Ponza, Her Son-in-Law."[4] The play pleased its author, who found it in "una originalità che grida,"[5] an originality that cries out. This originality is encased in Pirandello's most carefully constructed play, a play that not only employs but seems to insist upon the three-act structure of the well-made play.

The surface of *That's the Way Things Are* is thoroughly realistic. The play takes place in the drawing room of a comfortable bourgeois family, the Agazzis, and deals with the arrival of a trio of newcomers into a tightly knit social structure. The newcomers—Signor and Signora Ponza and Signora Frola, Signora Ponza's mother—cause suspicion because they do not live together, and more important, because Signora Frola will not receive the Agazzis when they come to call on her. Since the old woman lives in the same building as the Agazzis, and since Signor Agazzi is Signor Ponza's superior at work, a social snub has occurred.

As the Agazzis pursue their investigation into the reasons for the strange behavior of the Ponza-Frola family, they discover a puzzle. Signor Ponza claims that his wife is not really Signora Frola's daughter, but his second wife, who allows the old woman to continue in her belief that Ponza is still married to her daughter. Signora Frola counters by saying that Ponza treated his wife so badly that she had to be sent away, and that when she returned he would accept her only if she married him again and thus would be thought of as his second wife. The Agazzis become obsessed by their search to discover the "truth" of the matter so that they can determine which of the two persons is telling the truth and which, in their minds, is mad, suffering from a delusion that suggests insanity.

While the surface facts of the play suggest realism, its structure works in the opposite direction. This structure meticulously balances and repeats its action and confrontations. Each act follows the same pattern. The Agazzi family and their friends, increasing in number and ferocity as the play progresses, discuss the mysterious actions of the three outsiders. One member of this group, Signora Agazzi's brother, Lamberto Laudisi, challenges the assumptions and actions of the others, but fails to convince them of either the impropriety or the ultimate impossibility of the investigation they are conducting.[6]

After the introductory discussion among the Agazzi group, with Laudisi's objections as counterpoint, each act centers on a confrontation with one or more of the newcomers. In Act I the chorus, as the Agazzi circle is identified by both Bentley and the director of a recent Italian production,[7] meet first with Signora Frola, then with her son-in-law, Ponza, and then with Signora Frola again. In Act II the two are brought together so that their conflicting versions of reality can be resolved. When this ploy fails, since they have acted in a way that protects both stories, the third-act appearance of Signora Ponza is necessitated, with all three family members present to satisfy the town's desire to discover "the truth."

The final balancing aspect of the play's structure occurs at the curtain of each act, after the newcomers have left the stage and the fact-finding mission of the society has been thwarted. Now Laudisi, the man who has tried to dissuade them from their inquisition, mocks the results of their inquiry. At the end of the first act he says, "You're looking at each other's eyes? Ah, the truth?" For the second-act finale he says, "And thus, ladies and gentlemen, the truth is discovered." The play concludes with, "And thus, friends, that's how the truth speaks. Are you happy?" followed by the mocking laugh that has also closed the previous two acts.

The dramatic significance of the character of Laudisi, and his laughter that punctuates the end of each act, will be discussed later in this chapter. At this point, however, the question of the rationale behind Pirandello's symmetrical design of his play deserves to be explored. In the precise patterning of the three acts, Pirandello goes beyond the normal neatness of the well-made play to insist upon structure in a way that will cause his audience to become aware of it. A tension between the realism of the play's subject matter and the stylization of its structure is created, and out of this tension comes the signal for the way in which the entire play is to be viewed.

Although *That's the Way Things Are* does not overtly call attention to itself as a piece of theater, thereby placing itself in the tradition of Modernism as defined by Greenberg, it can be seen as a preliminary step in that direction. While it is *Six Characters in Search of an Author* that makes the break with realistic illusion, here the stylization and symmetry of form give the play a somewhat self-conscious feeling. The play thus seems poised precariously between realism and theatrical self-identification, partaking of certain aspects of theatrical tradition while suggesting an alternative to others.

Beyond this feeling that "things are not what they might appear to be," there is another clue that this play is to be taken humoristically as defined by Pirandello in his essay, moving beyond a surface reaction to a more complex way of apprehending reality. This clue can be found in his classification of the work as "parable, in truth, more than a play." [8] With the use of this term Pirandello suggests that he is less interested in the re-creation of reality or the illusion of reality on the stage, in the tradition of *verismo*, and more concerned with the exploration of larger truths that can be abstracted from the surface situation. Both in his identification of the play as parable, and more important, in his structuring of the play's action in such an obvious pattern, Pirandello is warning his audience that the play may not really be about what it appears to be about. The play's "truth" may not only lie well beneath the surface, but it may even be in contrast to what is suggested by that surface, just as the surface realism and the "artificial symmetry" of the structure are in conflict.

While the term "parable" does not suggest the *contrario,* or oppositeness, that is crucial to *umorismo,* it does point in the important direction of the movement beneath the surface. Although the characters and actions of a parable need not be seen totally as symbols, there is a larger, more generalized concept that is to be seen beneath the surface reality. There is also an educative purpose behind a parable, whereby a lesson with a general applicability can be deduced from the specific example of the incident. Pirandello is working in a similar way here, but in adapting the parable idea to his purposes, he adds the technique of *umorismo,* so that not only is the "truth" of his play to be deduced beneath its surface, but that "truth" may be the opposite of what the surface might at first suggest.

The surface of *That's the Way Things Are* is studded with the formulation of philosophical positions in such a way as to suggest that this is an intellectual play, dealing with the nature of reality and the possibility or impossibility of establishing a finite, knowable "truth." The triumph of Laudisi and the frustration of the chorus at the conclusion, when Signora Ponza affirms both of the conflicting positions of her husband and mother, would also seem to indicate the dramatization of an argument for relativism as the correct approach to life. There is no one knowable truth, and any attempt to establish such a position is bound to end in failure.

The entire structure of the play seems to lead up to Signora Ponza's appearance at the end of Act III, when—all assume—she will settle the question as to which version of her identity is correct. When she fails to deliver this resolution, the cry goes up that Pirandello is manipulating his play in order to establish his own intellectual position. Yet this final statement does not come as a thunderbolt. Earlier in the act, when Laudisi says that the wife is the only person who can clear up the mystery, his associates immediately identify this suggestion as the perfect solution. He issues a warning, however, that prepares the attentive audience member for the denouement of the play, while going unheeded by Laudisi's impetuously monomaniacal friends:

LAUDISI *(as if struck with a new idea):* Oh! But, excuse me, are you really sure that she exists?
AMALIA: What? My lord, Lamberto.
SIRELLI *(pretending to laugh):* Do you want us to doubt her very existence?
LAUDISI: All right, let us proceed slowly. You said yourselves that no one has ever seen her.
DINA: Go on. The old woman sees her and speaks with her every day.
SIGNORA SIRELLI: And even he says so, the son-in-law.
LAUDISI: Very well. But think about it for a minute. According to the rigors of logic must she not be only a phantom?
ALL: A phantom?
AGAZZI: Stop pulling our legs.
LAUDISI: Let me explain it to you. The phantom of a second wife, if she is right, Signora Frola. Or the phantom of a daughter, if he is the one who is right, Signor Ponza. Now it remains to be seen, friends, if this phantom, for either one of them or the other, is then a real person for herself. Having arrived at this point, it seems to be that there is real reason to doubt it.

The end of the play is thus not the surprise that the chorus, and those members of the audience who have been following the action from their point of view, might think it is. The lack of a resolution has been prepared for through the logic of Laudisi's position, but more important, through the psychological truth of the characters Pirandello has created and the antirealistic structure of his "parable."

The psychology of the three outsiders is particularly important, since it triggers the movement beyond the intellectual surface of the play. In the definition of the *avvertimento* and *sentimento* levels in *L'umorismo,* the former concerns itself primarily with the intellectual apprehension of the particular phenomenon, while the latter includes the emotional response as well. Of course Pirandello is dealing with ideas in *That's the Way Things Are,* but he is doing so in a way that begins an exploration of the connection between idea and feeling, thought and emotion, that will become one of the cornerstones of his dramaturgy. The chorus approaches the outsiders' dilemma on the purely *avvertimento* level, while the suffering of the three newcomers necessitates an approach that also takes into consideration the emotion of the *sentimento* response.

The ideas of *That's the Way Things Are* seem to be its focus because they are its most obvious feature. Just as the patterned structure acts as a warning against the easy acceptance of the realistic surface, with its red herring of the mystery aspect of the play, so the emotional reality of the Ponza-Frola family challenges the acceptance of the Agazzis' quest for "the truth." The intellectual-philosophical point about illusion and reality and the ability to establish certainty that Pirandello appears to be establishing is, therefore, ultimately much less important than the sociohumanitarian one about the need for compassion in dealing with the suffering of others. The key issue becomes, not whether the Agazzi family and their friends *can* find out the truth about the Ponza-Frola family, but whether they *should* be trying to do so. Philosophy yields to morality here, and it is a morality based on compassion that finally triumphs.[9] The play never makes the point that an objective reality does not or cannot exist. In fact, the existence of such a truth is acknowledged by the play. The chorus's quest is doomed to fail, however, because the three sufferers will do everything necessary to keep that truth hidden so they can protect each other and shield themselves from experiencing more pain.

In order to emphasize the emotional life of the play, the chorus and the triumvirate of sufferers move in opposite directions. As the chorus becomes more involved in the "mystery," its members take sides and develop personal stakes in the outcome. The entire social and political structure of the society becomes implicated in the solution of the Ponza-Frola controversy. Tension mounts, culminating in the third-act hysteria over a letter Laudisi produces, claiming that it supplies the objective facts necessary for the determination of "the truth." The arrival of the Commissioner and the Prefect widens the scope of the inquiry into the public realm. The increasing frenzy over proving the rectitude of one's position completely overwhelms the group of busybodies. If any concern for the feelings and well-being of the Ponza-Frola family ever existed, it has now been eradicated. They no longer exist as people for the inquisitive mob, for they have posed a problem, and it is the solution of that problem that now takes precedence.

As the humanity of the Ponza-Frola family is lost sight of by the

Agazzi circle, it is the Agazzis themselves who become less individualized as the play progresses. With the expansion of the group from act to act, the individual members become less important. In Act I Laudisi has dealt specifically with the Sirellis as individuals, and in Act II he held a conversation with Signora Cini and Signora Nenni. By Act III, however, even the individual members of the Agazzi family who began the probe are less important in themselves than as the threatening force they present en masse. It is no longer possible for the Ponza-Frola family to receive humane treatment, because individuality has been subordinated to the group effort to discover "the truth."

Just as in a war situation, where the original objectives often become blurred by and subordinated to the sheer desire for victory, here Pirandello carefully builds his play so that the characters searching for "the truth" become less and less interested in that truth itself and more and more concerned with their individual stakes in the result. The widening scope of the inquiry, to include public officials as well as curious gossips, creates a chasm between the investigators and the object of their inquiry. A power struggle has emerged, and the identification of Signora Frola or Signor Ponza as the person telling the truth is needed to vindicate the faction backing the "correct" position.

At the same time that the chorus is growing in number and becoming less individualized and less interested in humanitarian concerns, the plight of the three victims becomes more sharply experienced by the audience. Although the basic situation is established by the appearance of both Ponza and Signora Frola in Act I, it is really in the second act, when they are brought together and forced to play a very painful scene for the onlookers' behalf, that the effects of the investigation begin to have their real impact. The savageness with which Ponza must attack his mother-in-law so that they both can maintain their visions of reality begins the pattern of cruelty that is climaxed during the appearance of Signora Ponza in Act III. It is this cruelty, and its resultant suffering, that form the center of the play, and not the ideas that serve only as counterpoint to the emotional reality underneath.

Ponza challenges the chorus with the true nature of their inquiry, which he identified as an inquisition, when he reveals in Act III that he and his family have decided to leave the Agazzis' community rather than continue to endure the kind of harassment to which they have been subjected. As he enters he is described as evidencing "great unrest and acute agitation." After Ponza requests a transfer from the Prefect, saying that he has been subjected to "an unheard-of oppression," the Prefect suggests that he is exaggerating. When Signor Agazzi interrupts to ascertain if Ponza is referring to him, Ponza says the following:

> I'm referring to all of you. And that is why I am going away. I am leaving, Signor Prefect, because I cannot tolerate this relentless, ferocious inquisition into my private life, which will result in compromising and then irreparably damaging an act of charity that has cost me so much pain and so many sacrifices. I venerate that poor old woman more than a mother, and yesterday, here, I was forced to treat her with the cruelest kind of violence. Today I discovered her in such a state of humiliation and agitation. . . .

At this point Agazzi interrupts again, saying that the old woman appeared very calm, and that it is Ponza who is acting hysterically.

Agazzi has, of course, listened, but he has not really heard what Ponza is saying. Ponza is not trying to discredit his mother-in-law's story and reinforce his own, as Agazzi's purely intellectual interpretation suggests. Ponza is trying to avoid further pain. He has undertaken a difficult activity, but one to which he feels a real commitment. He seeks no congratulation for it. Yet it is impossible for him to achieve his desired mission of mercy when both he and Signora Frola are being subjected to a series of confrontations designed to break down their defenses and determine a "truth" that will destroy the arrangement they have worked so carefully to establish.

The idea of inquisition suggested by Ponza in this speech has been dramatically communicated by Pirandello from the initial interrogation of Signora Frola in Act I. She enters, apologizes for her failure to receive the Agazzi family when they came to call on her, and becomes immediately subjected to a barrage of questions that are far from friendly inquiries. Some of the questions are obviously tricks to test the veracity of the old woman's responses. The busybodies, moreover, refuse to stop with the information she volunteers, but insist on drawing her out. Dina, the Agazzis' daughter, says that she could never be content to communicate with her mother only by note, thus making it necessary for Signora Frola to say more and implicate her son-in-law in a manner she obviously wanted to avoid doing.

As the investigation into the Frola-Ponza relationship intensifies, so does the suffering caused by that inquiry. When Signora Frola enters the Agazzi home in Act III, the time is most inopportune. Ponza has been sent to bring his wife so that she can resolve the discrepancy in the two conflicting stories. He has agreed, on condition that Signora Frola not be present. Now the old woman has arrived unexpectedly, and the Agazzis and the Prefect try to convince her to leave:

PREFECT: No, please be patient, my dear woman. I cannot possibly listen to you right now. You must go away! You must leave this house immediately.

SIGNORA FROLA: Yes, I will go away. I will go away this very day. I will depart, Signor Prefect. I will make my departure from here forever.

AGAZZI: But no, signora. Please be good enough to wait for a few minutes next door in your apartment. Please do me this favor. Then you will be able to speak with the Prefect.

SIGNORA FROLA: But why? What is it? What's going on?

AGAZZI *(losing his patience):* Your son-in-law is about to return here. There—now do you understand?

SIGNORA FROLA: Ah! Yes? And then, yes . . . yes, I'll go, I'll go right away. I just wanted to tell you this one thing: for the sake of all that is holy, please finish with this. You all believe that you are doing me good, and instead you are doing great harm. I will be forced to go away if you continue to act in this way; to go away this very day, because he must be left in peace! But what do you want with him here now? What must he come here to do?—Oh, Signor Prefect!

PREFECT: Nothing, signora, be calm, please be calm and leave.

AMALIA: Please be good and go away, signora.

SIGNORA FROLA: Oh, God, signora, you will deprive me of my one happiness, of the only comfort that remains to me: to at least be able to see my daughter from a distance. *(She begins to cry.)*

PREFECT: But what are you talking about? You don't have to move

away—we are only asking you to leave this apartment for a few minutes. Please be calm.
SIGNORA FROLA: But I am worried about him, Signor Prefect. I came here to entreat you on his behalf, not mine.
PREFECT: Yes, very well. And you can rest assured also on his part. You will see that everything will be taken care of.
SIGNORA FROLA: But how? I see you all here, pursuing him relentlessly.
PREFECT: No, signora. That is not true. We are here for his benefit. Please try to calm yourself!
SIGNORA FROLA: Oh, thank you. Do you mean that you have understood . . . ?
PREFECT: Yes, yes, signora. I understand.
SIGNORA FROLA: I have repeated it over and over again to all these people: it is a tragedy that we have been able to overcome, something that is best not returned to.
PREFECT: Yes, very well, signora. . . . I assure you that I understand the situation.
SIGNORA FROLA: We are content to live this way; my daughter is content. Therefore—please let it end here, because if not, the only thing open to me would be to leave here and never see her again, not even as it is now, from a distance. . . . Leave him alone, for the love of God!

The conversation with Signora Frola is then interrupted by the sound of people arriving; and the final confrontation with Ponza, his wife, and Signora Frola is precipitated.

I have quoted this exchange at length for several reasons. One is to show Signora Frola's selflessness in her dealings with the Prefect and his compatriots. Her concern with her son-in-law's welfare is evidenced by the sacrifice she is willing to undertake in leaving her daughter. She has accepted the long-distance approach of visiting with her child as the one happiness in her tragedy-filled life, yet she is willing to give it up in order to save her son-in-law from the continued harassment of the chorus. Her selflessness is etched in sharp contrast to the curiosity of that group, who think first only of the slight that they have received, and then of their stake in determining who has correctly identified the person telling the true version of the story.

The anguish experienced by Signora Frola in this scene sets her apart from her interrogators. She directs her pleas to the Prefect because he has power the others lack and because he has not participated in their cruel examination of her life. Although he tries to placate her, his motives are suspect because he knows that the wife is about to arrive, and is therefore more intent on getting Signora Frola to leave than on reacting compassionately to her cry for assistance.

The depth of the old woman's pain as she pleads for the Prefect's assistance is indicated by his response to her. In less than a page of dialogue he tells her to calm herself five times, using the imperative form of the verb—"stia tranquilla." His nervousness over the imminent arrival of the Ponzas is not enough to justify this repetition. Signora Frola has been subjected to intense harassment. She is also a woman fighting for the right to remain with her daughter, and whether that woman is really her daughter or whether Signora Frola merely believes so makes no difference. Her back is against the wall, and her agitation is evidence of the commitment she has made to the two people in the world she has left to love.

Neither the Prefect nor the other members of the chorus of busybodies can truly understand Signora Frola here because they are trying to use the intellect in a situation in which the intellect should not dominate. As Pirandello has suggested in his image of the grotesque old woman of *L'umorismo,* it is necessary to go beyond first impressions, beneath the surface appearances to the emotional reality covered by the more easily comprehended facade. The apparent lie told by either Signora Frola or her son-in-law, motivated by either deceit or madness, becomes inconsequential when compared with the great tragedy these two people have experienced. They have been motivated by deep compassion, a compassion evident in their actions, but that has not been perceived by the "detectives" examining their lives. These "detectives" have so intellectualized the problem, so abstracted it from the reality of the people involved, that the individuals no longer exist as human beings. In perhaps the greatest irony of the play, the inquisitors, in their search for "the truth," are incapable of dealing with what is, in fact, the central truth of the three outsiders—their enormous suffering and the subsequent attempts to alleviate that suffering as much as possible with love.[10]

The anguish and accompanying compassion of the Ponza-Frola family makes Signora Ponza's statement at the end of the play, when she identifies herself as both Ponza's wife and Signora Frola's daughter, the only possible solution. Laudisi's statement at the beginning of Act III has prepared both the chorus and audience for this eventuality. Yet the chorus, and the members of the audience who have been caught up in the "mystery" aspect of the play, are still taken aback by the lack of a concrete solution. Why? The answer to this question leads to an examination of Pirandello's use of the theater and its devices as part of the aesthetic and intellectual content of the play.

In writing about the conflict between appearances and reality, Pirandello was not content to present the theme as an intellectual construct. Instead he structured his play in such a way that its surface is deliberately misleading. Members of the audience who follow the lead of the Agazzi family and concern themselves only with the superficial aspects of the Ponza-Frola family are going to be misled, just as the Agazzis are misled. The surface facts of the play, as well as the increase in dramatic tension, suggest that it is a mystery, with "who is lying?" as the central question. For those in the audience who have disregarded Laudisi's warnings and, more important, the misery inflicted on the old woman and her family, the end will frustrate them in the same way the investigators are frustrated.

Pirandello is not merely playing games with his audience by building this trap into the structure of his play. He wants to communicate the reality of suffering and the need for compassion, as well as the dangerous effects idle curiosity and prying can have. For the audience members who see that the identity of who is telling the truth cannot or should not be sought, Pirandello does not need to do anything further. But what about the others, the Agazzis and Sirellis and prefects of the audience who do not pay attention to either intellectual warnings or emotional pleas? Pirandello must make these people experience a frustration that may ultimately lead to the intellectual and emotional realization of why it was necessary for the play to end as it does.

Pirandello is playing with contraries here. He is also beginning to experiment with ways he can use the theater and the relationship between his characters onstage and the audience to communicate the richness of these contraries. The stage still creates the illusion of a bourgeois salon, and not the theater itself. Yet his experiment with the use of realistic surface detail to create an identity between audience and character that will ultimately be frustrated if the audience has not followed his play carefully suggests an awareness that he is working in a nonliterary medium, a medium dependent on an audience's immediate response to what is presented before them.

It is ironic that this play is often criticized as too obvious a dramatization of Pirandello's ideas, an overintellectualized piece that places too much emphasis on ideas. It is indeed the very segment of Pirandello's audience approaching this play intellectually, as a mystery to be solved by the assembling of clues and careful interrogation of witnesses, that shares the frustration of the chorus at the play's end. They have missed the "reality" of the play and have been duped by the red herrings of the trappings of realism and a structure that builds to a "solution" that does not satisfy.

The suffering of Ponza and Signora Frola is the crux of the play, and this suffering is expressed in painfully realistic, almost melodramatic terms. Those in the audience who have not responded to their cries to call off the violent inquisition threatening to destroy the delicate fabric of their accommodation with life must be made aware of their insensitivity. By giving them a conclusion contrary to their expectations, Pirandello can suggest the danger of overintellectualizing and stopping at the surface that is the theme, not only of *L'umorismo*, but of his drama as well.

Pirandello complicates and enriches his play by adding a third participant in the conflict between the chorus of busybodies and the triumvirate of newcomers. This individual, who stands between and among the others and is both essential and in a paradoxical way superfluous to the struggle for power and information in which they are engaged, is Lamberto Laudisi. Laudisi is often considered the play's central figure, the *raisonneur* character who acts as Pirandello's spokesman, espousing the author's philosophical position, especially his ideas on the impossibility of establishing one knowable truth.

It is impossible to deny Laudisi's importance to the surface of the play. He engages in important arguments with his sister's family and their coterie of friends, and comments with both words and laughter at the end of each act when their search for the truth has been frustrated. He argues for the privacy of the Ponza-Frola family and also suggests that even the appearance of Signora Ponza may not supply the verification they are seeking. He is the only member of the community seen onstage who is not enveloped in the witch hunt that swallows up the other characters. In the end, however, he is a figure who makes sense and yet is ineffectual, who seems to have all the answers and who really does not, who seems central and yet is peripheral to the drama of the three sufferers that is being acted out.

From the play's outset, Laudisi opposes his family and their friends in their harassment of Signor Agazzi's new co-worker and his family. Whereas Signora Agazzi and her daughter see Signora Frola's refusal to admit them into her home as a social outrage, Laudisi defends her right to privacy. He also forces them to admit that their social call was motivated by curiosity as well as hospitality. When Signor and Signora Sirelli arrive with Signora Cini, thirsting for the latest news, Laudisi tries to nip the investigation in the bud by convincing the assembly that what they are searching for cannot and should not be pursued.

Laudisi announces that his associates' curiosity should be curbed, if for no other reason than because it is useless, futile. "What can we possibly really know about others? Who they are.... How they are.... What they are doing.... Why they are doing it...?" he asks. Such abstractions convince no one, so Laudisi moves to illustrate his point. He behaves one way with Sirelli, then another with Sirelli's wife, hinting that he has romantic intentions toward her. He then suggests that while each of them sees him differently, for himself he remains the same. The crucial exchange occurs in the following lines:

SIGNORA SIRELLI: And therefore do you change from one to the other?
LAUDISI: But I am sure that I change, signora mia! And you do not, perhaps. You do not change?
SIGNORA SIRELLI *(precipitously):* Ah, no, no, no, no. I assure you that for myself I do not change at all.
LAUDISI: And in my eyes neither do I, believe me. And I say that

you are all deceiving yourselves if you do not look on me as I see myself. But this does not prevent it from being as great a presumption on my part as it is on yours, dear signora.
SIRELLI: Excuse me, but all of this sophistry, where does it lead?
LAUDISI: It doesn't seem to lead anywhere? Oh, fine. You seem worried, trying to find out who others are and what is the nature of things, almost as if other people and certain things were, in themselves, either one way or the other.
SIGNORA SIRELLI: But according to you then we can never know the truth?
SIGNORA CINI: As if we should no longer even believe in the things we see or touch ourselves.
LAUDISI: But of course you can believe them, signora. However, I am saying this: Respect what others see and touch, even if it is the opposite of what you see and touch.
SIGNORA SIRELLI: Listen, I'm turning my back and do not want to speak with you any longer. I do not want to become crazy.

The importance of this exchange lies not only in Laudisi's ideas but also in the way he expresses those thoughts. He is trying to discourage the public pursuit of private facts by showing the impossibility of establishing the nature of those facts. He is not saying that objective reality does not exist but that people see things in different ways. One must respect those ways of seeing, even if they do not coincide with one's own particular view. Laudisi is preaching tolerance, so that the key word in his argument is "respect." Yet he couches his argument in such abstract intellectual terms that he fails to communicate with his associates, so confusing them that they are unable to grasp the import of his words and dismiss him as directing them toward madness.

That's the Way Things Are has sometimes been criticized as a play in which the ideas are not fully expressed through the dramaturgy. Pirandello, it is said, has created a spokesman who presents the author's ideas to the audience so they cannot possibly miss his main points. While this may be true to some extent, one could still miss the point if not alert. A careful examination of Laudisi, however, and particularly the role he assumes in the play, suggests that Pirandello has done more with him than create a personal representative who states the "author's message." [11]

Throughout *That's the Way Things Are* Laudisi plays the role of the bemused, detached devil's advocate. He argues with the chorus and does so with logic, irony, and insight. He tries to convince them that their endeavor is bound to fail, that the Ponza-Frola family does not want to become known and will probably take actions that will make the establishment of the truth impossible. He also argues that their privacy should be respected. He always does so, however, in abstracted arguments that are tempered, not with appeals to compassion, but with his skeptical humor. Even when he is making points with both intellectual and emotional validity, his irony and bemused detachment make it easy for the chorus to dismiss him and continue their investigation.

Just as Pirandello builds the obsessive curiosity of the busybodies and the anguish of the victims, he also structures the revelation of Laudisi's detachment and ultimate ineffectuality, so that it is perceived bit by bit. In the first act, in fact, Signora Frola sees that he is sympathetic to her position and tries to enlist his articulateness to explain and justify her position. Realizing that it is her separation from her daughter that has caused the neighbors' suspicions, she immediately tries an obvious means of escape: "But, you know, it is only right, when a son or daughter gets married, that they should be left to themselves, to lead their own lives." Laudisi now enters the conversation for the first time since her arrival:

LAUDISI: Excellent. You could not have acted more correctly. Of course there must be a new, different kind of relationship with the wife or the husband.
SIGNORA SIRELLI: But not up to the point, excuse me Laudisi, of excluding the mother from their life.
LAUDISI: But who said exclude? We are talking now—if I heard right—about a mother who understands that her daughter can not and should not remain tied to her as she was before, now having another life that she is involved with.
SIGNORA FROLA *(with lively acknowledgment):* Exactly, it is just like that, ladies and gentlemen! Thank you! That is exactly what I meant to say.

The way in which Signora Frola jumps at Laudisi's defense suggests that she sees him as a possible champion of her cause, a perceptive and articulate man who can assist her in her troubles. He does not say anything more during the continuation of this interrogation, however, and in fact offers no further assistance to either the old woman or her son-in-law in their confrontations with the chorus, even when it is obvious that they are being subjected to intense harassment. When he does challenge the inquisitors in the absence of the newcomers, it is on intellectual rather than on emotional-humanitarian grounds. Laudisi mocks and cajoles the Agazzi circle but does nothing to assist or shield the victims when they are under attack.

What point does Pirandello seem to be making with his character of Laudisi? His mocking laugh at the end of each act, along with his ironic playing with the chorus, especially with two of his sister's friends in Act II, suggests an amusement at their activities. He sees their folly, tries to point it out to them, and at the same time realizes that they will not listen to him and will learn only from the eventual frustration of their investigation. He mocks their efforts but never makes a concerted effort to stop them. He realizes that his skepticism makes him easy to dismiss, but does not attempt another strategy that might convince the busybodies of the disastrous consequences their interference might have.

There is no doubt that Laudisi is a comic figure, a jokester and provider of merriment. As noted earlier, the structure of the play is so carefully fashioned as to call attention to itself. It is significant, therefore, that at the very center of the play, the middle of Act II, lies a truly comic scene, the one piece of sustained comic writing found in the entire play.[12]

Laudisi has been left alone while his relatives and their friends are off arranging the confrontation between Signora Frola and Ponza. He has tried to convince them that their insistence on establishing the truth of one of the two versions may not be so easy as they expect, but has been ignored, as he usually is. Alone on stage, and almost as a prelude to the scene that will follow, Laudisi sees himself in a mirror and conducts the following "conversation" with his image:

Oh, there you are. Now, dear friend—which one of us is the crazy one? *(He raises his hand with the index finger pointing at his image, which, from his viewpoint, points his finger at him. He laughs, then continues.*) Ah, I know. I say it is you and with your finger you point at me. It is all right that it appears this way for us, because we two know each other very well. The trouble is that the others do not see you the same way I do. And then, dear friend, what happens to you? I say that as far as I am concerned, when I look at you here I see and touch myself in seeing and touching you. But how do the others see you? As a phantom, dear friend, as a phantom. Now do you understand these madmen? Without considering the phantoms they carry with them, in themselves, they go running off, full of curiosity, in search of the phantoms of others. And they think that it is an entirely different matter.

Laudisi understands the insanity of what his family and their friends are trying to do. This understanding is expressed, however, in abstract terms, with the emphasis still on the busybodies themselves and not on the innocent people who will suffer.

The emphasis on madness in Laudisi's speech is a significant part of the play's overall design. The chorus of gossips' primary quest is the determination of whether Ponza or Signora Frola is mad. There is no doubt but that one of them must be. As the play suggests, however, the true insanity resides in their fanatical search for a "truth" that does not exist and does not affect them. Laudisi certainly does not suffer from their distorted perception, yet as I will argue in the conclusion of this chapter, his position is a tremendously ambiguous one. In the ultimate determination of the play, therefore, the three sufferers are sane; the gossips are the "crazy" ones; and Laudisi, poised in front of his mirror, inhabits the twilight zone between lucidity and madness.

Madness is not an abstract phenomenon for Pirandello, as it is for Laudisi and the "chorus." As a child he was preoccupied with images of madness and death. His younger sister was stricken with an illness that seemed to derange her during adolescence. Then, in 1903, his wife, Antonietta, became mentally ill when an earthquake destroyed the sulfur mines that had been the basis of her arranged marriage to Pirandello. Antonietta recovered from the initial effects of her illness; but a rabid, maniacal jealousy remained, and "she began to besiege her husband without pause, every moment of the day." [14] Since the tragedy of the Ponza-Frola family was also initiated by an earthquake, perhaps an analogy can be drawn between the situation in the play and Pirandello's life. As his literary fame increased, he would have to deal with a public anxious to learn more about his private life. For the curious outsider, Antonietta's mental condition might be cause for speculation and gossip; for Pirandello and his three children it was a burning, passionate problem, the great tragic burden of his life, demanding the sympathy of the *sentimento* response rather than the intellectual curiosity of the *avvertimento* level.

As soon as Laudisi concludes his speech to his mirror image, the butler enters to announce the arrival of two friends of Signora Agazzi. One of them, Signora Cini, has taken part in the first-act interrogation and has now brought Signora Nenni to swell the ranks of the circle questing for "the truth." In the absence of his sister, Laudisi receives the two women, seats himself between them, and proceeds playfully to mock and confuse them. He teases them as coconspirators about to be initiated into a great truth (the confrontation between Signora Frola and Ponza), then confuses them further by revealing that the second marriage between the Ponzas is indeed a fact. Since both versions of the story use the occurrence of a second marriage, differing on the crucial point of the identity of the bride, he has told them nothing that adds to their knowledge of the situation.

Laudisi then suggests that even if documentary evidence were discovered, the person whose story it damaged could argue that the documents were false. The two women are now thoroughly confused, and the following exchange concludes the scene:

SIGNORA CINI: But, then, oh, God, there is nothing we can be certain about.
LAUDISI: How can you say that? Do not exaggerate. Pardon me, how many days of the week are there?
SIGNORA CINI: Eh, seven.
LAUDISI: Monday, Tuesday, Wednesday ...
SIGNORA CINI *(encouraged to continue):* Thursday, Friday, Saturday.
LAUDISI: And Sunday *(turning to the other).* And the months of the year?
SIGNORA NENNI: Twelve.
LAUDISI: January, February, March ...

SIGNORA CINI: We get it. You're making fun of us.

Laudisi demolishes his adversaries by extending their interpretations of his ideas to the absurdest reduction. He is not saying that an individual cannot be certain of anything but that one must be prepared for the possibility that someone else will view the same phenomenon differently. And, as he argued in Act I, it is necessary to respect the other person's vision, even if it is incompatible with one's own. It is thus perception, and not the objective phenomenon itself, that partakes of relativism.

This comic scene, illustrating Laudisi's virtuosity and quickness of mind, stands at the center of the play in order to emphasize Pirandello's ridicule of the insensitive busybodies who want "the truth" at any cost. The scene's centrality may also suggest, however, Laudisi's main orientation in the play. He is perceptive, but he turns his perceptions in the direction of irony rather than compassion. Both of the women here are fools, perhaps even more foolish than the other chorus members. Laudisi still chooses to dazzle them with his intellectual gymnastics, befuddling them for his own amusement, rather than to convince them of the possible consequences of their behavior. Just like the people he mocks, he also has lost sight of the suffering at the heart of the play's dilemma.

Laudisi's actions in Act III clarify Pirandello's ambiguous use of this character. The chorus has reached a state of near hysteria, hungry for the smallest scrap of information about the Ponza-Frola family. Laudisi plays with this state of mind when he tells them that he has read a letter that purports to offer new facts about the case. His "facts," however, turn out to be information that was either previously known or is so ambiguous as to be useless in establishing definite proof.

Laudisi's suggestion that the investigation be dropped, since most of the chorus believes Signora Frola anyway, is rejected because the Prefect believes Ponza's version. It is at this point Laudisi offers the logical suggestion of bringing Signora Ponza before their "tribunal." The chorus has been so involved in the hysterical search for facts that this obvious idea has not occurred to them. While some objections are raised, the consensus is that this is the only solution possible, and Laudisi is saluted with bravos by all.

Laudisi now asks the crucial question, "are you sure that she exists?" By arguing that according to the rigors of logic Signora Ponza cannot exist for herself, he is preparing both his associates and the audience for the final revelation and its accompanying frustration. Yet his logic here is pure intellectualism. He has decided that it is time to stop the game once and for all. He will prove the validity of his thesis by offering what should be the resolution but that instead will be the ultimate frustration. He will checkmate his opponents, win the game, and have the last laugh.

Laudisi is falling into the same trap that has ensnared the chorus. He is ignoring the suffering that his "solution" may cause the Ponza-Frola family. He appears to be concerned only with his own circle of acquaintances and his revenge on them for their failure to heed his warnings. Laudisi's logic has completely taken over. A problem has been explored and not resolved, and now the only possible logical step is the appearance of Signora Ponza. He is taking into account the probable effect on the chorus but not the possible psychic damage such a scene might have on Signora Frola or Ponza. While he expects Signora Ponza to have no identity of her own, he cannot be sure. More important, he does not even consider the possible trauma that could be caused if she does disown her own identity in exchange for the dual identity that has been imposed upon her.

In other words, like the chorus he so scorns, Laudisi never seems to move from the *avvertimento* to the *sentimento* level. He has insights into the psychic needs of the characters involved and thus anticipates the arrangement they have reached. He even tries to warn the chorus of the eventuality he expects. Yet Laudisi never makes the leap to the *sentimento* level of perception because he never opposes the inquisition on the proper humanitarian grounds, on the grounds that what the chorus is doing may destroy three human beings who have suffered greatly already and who now may be attempting their last possible arrangement for survival together.

Although it is clear that the chorus and those people in the audience who are caught up in the "mystery" aspect of the play are not sympathetic to the crisis faced by the Ponza-Frola family, I think that Pirandello attributes the same limitation to Laudisi. He may be more intelligent than the people he scorns, but he never makes a concerted effort either to stop their investigation or to disassociate himself from it either by protesting vehemently in the name of decency or by leaving the drawing room. Laudisi stands apart from his sister and her associates because of the insights he has, but in other ways he stands with them in that he is more concerned with exercising his curiosity than in showing compassion for the suffering of others.

Laudisi's acquiescence in the continued violence his compatriots wreak on the three outsiders and the reprise of his sardonic laugh at the end of the final act identify him as uncommitted intellectual rather than as a compassionate observer. All of this must be conjecture, however, since Laudisi is the one unmotivated character in the play. While Pirandello makes the intentions of the chorus of busybodies and the triumvirate of victims clear, he creates Laudisi to stand as an outsider, a man of mystery who observes and comments, participating only in the making of suggestions and the mocking of failure. His attitude toward his associates is clear, but his attitude toward the newcomers is not, although it is hinted that he may be less interested in their plight than in the ultimate frustration it will cause those who are prying into it.

The ambiguity of Laudisi's actions and attitudes is a puzzling aspect of this play. Pirandello does not waste this ambiguity, however, but uses it as an echo of the play's central mystery. Just as the "reality" of the Ponza-Frola situation is unknowable because of the pact that the three have made, so Laudisi cannot really be known because he refuses to reveal himself. He has been talking about the difficulty of really knowing other people, about the fact that an individual can appear differently to different observers. Pirandello illustrates this point dramatically by having the character who espouses this position present such a problem for the audience.

While Laudisi may be the observer in the play who seems to see most clearly, Pirandello is suggesting that such perspicuity may not be sufficient. Laudisi does not allow his thoughts to deepen into feelings, and in focusing on the victimizers rather than on the victims, he misses the real tragedy of the play and settles instead for irony. Because his motives are not given, Laudisi must be judged by his actions; and his failure to intuit the emotional truth of the situation leads to the condemnation Pirandello implicitly suggests.

It is indeed ironic that *That's the Way Things Are* is often judged a philosophical or intellectual play. In fact, it presents an extremely strong case for the limitations of the intellect in dealing with certain situations, specifically where emotional suffering is involved. Although on the surface Laudisi seems to be fighting the inquisition pursued by his compatriots, he remains as much of an outsider to the Ponza-Frola family as the others. He is the detached comic observer in a situation where it is necessary to go further and feel the suffering beneath the surface. Once that suffering is felt, it is impossible to laugh at, or remain a detached observer of, the unspeakable cruelties inflicted by the chorus. By remaining an outsider himself, Laudisi becomes a part of the society he mocks. He does not share in their intellectual myopia, but his intellectuality also has its limitations, since he cannot transcend it to feel the agony of the three victims.

Pirandello's criticism, not only of those who pursue in idle curiosity, but also of those who stand on the sidelines and intellectualize and mock, stuns us with its perceptiveness, especially since we may have been caught up with the approach taken either by Laudisi or the chorus. We are stunned, moreover, because Pirandello has written neither a tract nor a straightforward elucidation of the problem. The pain generated by the Ponza-Frola family is so searing precisely because it is ignored by everyone else on the stage. What should have been a melodramatic mystery has been subverted into a tragedy, the tragedy of a family who has first been made to suffer by the blind exigencies of human nature, then by nature in the form of an earthquake, and now by the foolish curiosity of unwitting tormenters.

Can a tragedy end in mocking laughter? The answer here must be affirmative. The laughter is necessary because the tragedy just presented has possibly been missed. It has certainly been missed by the Agazzi clan and their "superior," Laudisi, and possibly also by at least part of the audience. For those who have not felt the tragedy communicated by the *sentimento del contrario*, Laudisi's laugh serves as a final jolt, an attempt to suggest that there is more than frustrated curiosity here. For those who have made the humoristic leap, the laughter reminds them that there are many people who have not, and that those people are dangerous, either actively, like the Agazzis, or passively, like Laudisi.

In the end, with its laugh commenting on the play and shocking its audience into recognition, Pirandello's "parable" comments on itself. More than a play dramatizing the inability to know "the truth" about others, or even the need to respect their visions, *That's the Way Things Are* ultimately becomes the parable expression of *umorismo* itself, not as a literary-critical process to probe beneath the surface of a work of art, but as an approach to life. Pirandello's parable preaches the need to search beneath all surfaces, to find the "reality" that may be lurking there. Pirandello has done this here, both formally in going beyond realism, and thematically in suggesting that a mystery may not have a solution and that even a *raisonneur* may not have all the answers.

3.

Six Characters in Search of an Author (1921)

The theater is the perfect medium for Pirandello's artistic expression. What better place to deal with illusion, pretense, and role playing than in the theater, where actors assume a role for an audience that accepts them as those characters and yet is also aware of their existence as actors? What better place to present an artistic vision epitomized by an old lady with excessive makeup and inappropriate clothes than the theater, where she is not merely described but is given life and appears before us? She may be the creation of an artistic imagination, but because she exists in front of us and not merely in the mind's eye, our laughter at her folly and our compassion for her pain will be both more immediate and more deeply felt.

In *The Theatre of Revolt,* Robert Brustein identifies the source of Pirandello's attraction to the theater in the following way:

> of all the literary forms, only the theatrical art combines the spontaneous and accidental with the ordered and predetermined. In the interplay between actors, audience and script, life and form merge. The living nature of theatrical art is

further exemplified by its immediacy ... the drama takes place in the present with nothing separating the speaker from the speech. If anything written is fixed and dead, and literary characters are like the figures in Yeats's *Purgatory*—doomed to eternal repetition of their torments—then anything staged is subject to accident, whim and change, the actors insuring that it will always be new.[1]

This immediacy is crucial to the communication of Pirandello's vision, for it is when an audience's attention is strongly engaged that it will be more likely to probe beyond the surface to discover the reality underneath. The complexity of the art form itself (the interplay of actors, audience, and script) will be more conducive to a complexity of response, with that response combining thought and emotion to perceive what may well contradict the initial, more limited reaction.

The reconciliation of life and form Brustein discusses is only one reason for Pirandello's choice of the theater as his means of expression. Moreover, the theater's combination of the spontaneity of life with the formal restrictions of art suggests their interpenetration rather than their existence as dialectical opposites. Dramatic art has form, of course, but within that form of the fixed script, change is not only possible but inevitable. Although it is true that the perception of any piece of nonperformed art varies from one person to the next as well as from generation to generation, the work itself is frozen after the artist completes it.

The differences in presentations of the same play are not only the result of the accident and whim suggested by Brustein. Each performance of a given production will vary from the ones that preceded and those that will follow. The intangible relationship between actor and audience allows the performers to sense a receptivity to their work at certain performances that may spur them on, both as individuals and as an ensemble, to new refinements and achievements. On the other hand, technical malfunctions, fatigue, and other external factors may have adverse effects on a particular evening's performance.

Yet from one production to another of the same play even greater changes occur. A new group of actors, director, and designers makes a different interpretation of the text, presenting another vision of the same words and characters. Something new can be found in the script, or a forgotten aspect can be recaptured. Because the audience in the theater is seeing the play through the lens offered by the production, what it ultimately views is a combination of the form created by the playwright and the life breathed into it by the interpreters. When this combination is achieved successfully, the two parts merge into a totally integrated unit, where the final result is more important than its individual components. And just as in the theater the play never can be seen "naked," without interpreters, so in life we can know someone else only through the way he appears and the way we perceive him.

The collective nature of an audience's theatrical experience is another important connection between the content of Pirandello's plays and his choice of medium. His use of *umorismo* extends beyond its application to the individual and encompasses the way in which people in groups (like the chorus in *That's the Way Things Are*) react to the predicaments of others.[2] With a dramaturgy that attempts to induce one kind of response only to then encourage its opposite, Pirandello can make the group of people that constitute his audience more aware of their responses as members of a group as well as individually. By encouraging this awareness, moreover, he can alert them to the extent to which they share a common humanity with others, a humanity that demands attention to more than the surface aspects of reality, a humanity that demands the use of emotion as well as intellect.

It is almost inevitable, therefore, that Pirandello eventually includes the audience as an actual part of one of his plays, *Each in His Own Way*. Differences in perception and complexity of vision are dominant themes, not only of Pirandello's work, but of much of the art of his day. The novels of Marcel Proust, James Joyce, Italo Svevo, and Virginia Woolf and the painting and sculpture of the Cubists and Futurists are examples of a general insistence on seeing the world in terms of complexity and multiplicity of image.[3] But the theatrical audience not only sees interpretation and text merging into one entity but must make individual judgments and analysis while at the same time sharing responses with a group of largely unknown people. The response of the audience thus becomes one more aspect of the theatrical experience that reflects the ideas being dramatized.

Pirandello's attraction to the theater can also be partly explained by his national background. Much of Italian life, especially its more passionate side, has a basic and undeniable theatricality. It is not accidental that one of Italy's greatest contributions to theater is the commedia dell'arte, with its emphasis on spontaneity, immediacy, and broad physical actions. Anyone who watches Italians in conversation soon realizes that the hands, and indeed the entire body, often communicate as much as the words these gestures accompany. The outsider can easily mistake a simple conversation for a heated argument, since many Italians converse with a commitment and excitement that is often not commensurate with the importance of the subject matter. This gesticulation and the spirit it expresses are theatrical, if not operatic, suggesting a performance even when none is intended by the participants.

In describing one of his characters, Mauri in *Come prima, meglio di prima (As Before, Better than Before)*, Pirandello illustrates his belief that many of man's actions are basically theatrical:

> in his forties, dark, thin, with lucid and mobile eyes like those of a lunatic; almost joyous even in the deepest agitation, expressive. He speaks and gestures with that theatricality that is characteristic of an exalted passion, a theatricality warm and sincere, but which at times is conscious of itself to the point of almost seeing itself.[4]

There are two basic qualities of Mauri's theatricality. One is its agitation, expressiveness, warmth, and sincerity, the kind of theatricality Pirandello himself observed as he grew up in Sicily and that he later captured in plays like *Liolà* and *The Jar*. The other quality is the consciousness, the awareness to the point of self-observation. Pirandello realizes that a character's theatricality need not be unexamined or unconscious but that it can be used by its possessor for certain ends. In fact, he uses the theater self-consciously in the same way, to examine itself and its relationship to life. Just as the masks and illusions of life need to be examined, with the assistance of the humorist who probes beneath their surface, so in the same way the theater, the mirror of human actions as well as the source of what it sometimes reflects, must be examined at the same time it is being used to communicate insights into the human activities it imitates.

Thus, in the plays that are usually referred to as his theater trilogy—*Six Characters in Search of an Author (Sei personaggi in cerca d'autore)*, *Each in His Own Way*, and *Tonight We Improvise*—Pirandello pushes the theater into Modernism by attempting such an exploration of the theatrical process and its relationship to the world it mirrors. Although the three plays were not composed as a trilogy in the usual sense, with continuity of either chronology [5] or plot and character, they form a unity because each is set in the theater and takes the theatrical experience as its subject matter as well as its major metaphor for the author's vision of life.

All three of the theater trilogy plays break through the imaginary "fourth wall" of the realistic theater in an attempt to destroy the barrier between auditorium and stage. Although each play includes many of the participants in the theatrical process, the focus of each work is on one of the three essential components of that process. *Six Characters* emphasizes the subject matter, the characters whose script is dramatized on stage; *Each in His Own Way*, the audience that views the theatrical presentation; and *Tonight We Improvise*, the actors who interpret the script and bring it to life for the audience. Despite this difference in perspective for each play, the trilogy as a whole becomes the examination of the relationship between theater art and life, and the interdependence and interpenetration of the two. Through *umorismo*, after a surface reality has been created the contradictions that lie hidden beneath it are explored, contradictions that can be apprehended only by a vision that combines intellect and feeling.

With *Six Characters in Search of an Author*, Pirandello made a sharp break with his previous work. Although he had suggested alternative ways of viewing reality and truth in *That's the Way Things Are* and some of his subsequent plays, he had done so within a fairly realistic framework. Only after he had made his audience comfortable with the customary theatrical trappings of the day did he unveil his experiments. In *Six Characters*, Pirandello goes beyond these modifications by eliminating the familiar milieu. The audience enters the auditorium to a raised curtain revealing a bare stage. When the "play" begins, actors and other stage personnel appear dressed in everyday clothes and begin chatting casually among themselves. Then a rehearsal of an old Pirandello play begins, instead of the new work that had been anticipated.

Pirandello attacks the customary stage realism in a very peculiar way. Instead of presenting his alternative vision by dramatizing states of the subconscious or creating images of pure fantasy, as other experimenters of the time did, he works in the opposite direction, insisting on an absolute realism, a realism the original audience was unwilling to accept. This audience, as seen by their violent reaction at the play's premiere,[6] apparently did not want to be reminded that they were seated in a theater. Instead they desired to be transported out of that reality into the illusion of a new reality, with a new environment and new characters whose problems they could become involved with. They paradoxically wanted "realism" in order to escape. Pirandello, on the other hand, gave them "reality" in order to confront them with insights about themselves and their lives.

Throughout the theater trilogy the audience is shown that just as the human personality and objective truth are no longer monolithic and easily knowable, so reality shares in this same multiplicity. One way to suggest this complexity of reality is to break down old distinctions that were previously accepted without examination. Since he is a writer in the theater, it is natural for Pirandello to turn toward the theater itself and examine it in a new way. Instead of accepting the old separation between the actors on stage and the audience in the auditorium, he seeks to create a unity between the two. Not only is the stage acknowledged as stage, but actors actually leave the proscenium frame and enter the auditorium. Instead of focusing on how theater can be like life (the assumption on which realism is based), he concentrates on how life can imitate theater, and how the two can come together so that the distinction between them can be made only with extreme difficulty. He also shows how people use the apparatus of the theater—role playing, masks, costumes, and so on—to structure their lives and the responses of others to those lives.

In *That's the Way Things Are* there is an insistence on the play's three-act structure so that the form will come into collision with the superficial reality of the "mystery." In *Six Characters* the desire to suggest that his audience is not really watching a play but an encounter between two groups in a theater leads Pirandello in the opposite direction. There is a mystery here also—is the Father or the Stepdaughter correct?—but Pirandello covers his tracks so that the audience remains unaware of the artistic formulation of the piece and concentrates on the immediacy and reality of the confrontation taking place.

In several ways *Six Characters* is a logical extension of *That's the Way Things Are*. In both plays outsiders try to communicate their problems to an established group and fail, demonstrating, in the process, not only the difficulty of human communication but also the barriers that people erect in order to resist a new, more complex mode of perception. Both plays also end with a lack of resolution and certainty. Yet *Six Characters*, by abandoning the drawing room and obvious three-act structure that could have been used to present the characters' "story," adds a new dimension to Pirandello's explorations. By acknowledging the theatrical setting of his play, he juxtaposes the perceptions and illusions of art with those of life, establishing both their parallels and their divergences.

In moving beyond the artificial formulation of the traditional realistic play, Pirandello does not designate the three sections of *Six Characters* as acts. Beyond this lack of demarcation, moreover, he does not force these sections to build to an artificial climax, but permits the conclusion of each part to appear as a natural break in the play's action. On the other hand, the basic separation of the play into three portions remains. Even when Pirandello is more experimental than his audience wants him to be, he does not flaunt tradition (he still allows them to have their two intermissions) but merely adjusts it to fit his own purposes.

After the actors' rehearsal has been interrupted by the arrival of six characters who have been abandoned by their playwright-creator, the first part concludes when the characters finally convince the company's director to dramatize their story. He must now develop a script with them and discuss the project further, so he gives the actors a fifteen-minute break. Everyone leaves the stage, but the curtain remains raised. A natural pause has occurred without the playwright's needing an artifice to break his play. The natural intermission in the activities on stage also allows the audience to take a pause. Here form has become a natural outgrowth of content, with no need to call attention to itself.

The conclusion of the second act may be more obvious than the first, but it still is a logical outgrowth of the play's action. The critical confrontation between the Father and the Stepdaughter in Madam Pace's salon has finally been concluded and then repeated by the actors. The Director is pleased with the resolution of the scene, but the Father insists that what has just been presented are real events, not merely an artistic formulation. The Director agrees, saying, "But of course, what else? Curtain! Curtain!" to signify that the scene is over. At this point a stagehand actually lowers the curtain, separating the Father and Director, who are in front of it, from the rest of the company. As the two men rejoin the rest of the company behind the curtain, the "second act" has been completed.

The conclusion of the big scene between the Father and Stepdaughter presents a natural opportunity for a pause. The use of the curtain, however, for the first and only time in the play, makes several significant points. One is a reminder of the theatrical tradition being violated. Another is the isolation of the Father and Director from the rest of the company and characters. This visually enforces what the rest of the play makes clear: that the central conflict of the play is theirs and that they stand apart from the rest of their associates.

The stagehand's error in interpretating literally the Director's metaphoric call for "Curtain" is also significant, especially in light of one of the Father's earlier speeches. There he had argued that the different meanings each person assigns to words makes communication difficult, if not impossible. The Director has dismissed the Father's statement as pointless intellectualizing. Now the literal interpretation of the Director's metaphor proves the validity of the Father's viewpoint, an insight that is also affirmed by the obvious difficulties encountered when the characters and the theater company attempt to communicate with each other.

The central conflict of *Six Characters* is summed up in the continuing clashes between the Father and the Director. This conflict is between two different ways of seeing, two different approaches to life. There are similarities to the struggle between the chorus and the newcomers in *That's the Way Things Are,* but the conflict is less orderly in *Six Characters,* with the accompanying chaos constituting an important aspect of the play. The mistaken lowering of the curtain is part of this sense of chaos, foreshadowing the end of "Act III," when the entire relationship between the characters and the theater company collapses in the controversy over the reality of the deaths of the two young children. The fragmentation of the conclusion, with actors, the Director, and even the Stepdaughter fleeing from the stage, reinforces the chaos of interpersonal relationships and the fragmentation of knowable reality that has been dramatized throughout, in both content and structure. The conclusion is thus consistent with what has preceded it by refusing to supply the kind of certainty that much of the audience would welcome with gratitude and relief.

It would be an oversimplification to assert that this play dramatizes a conflict between the old and the new, and yet the six characters do bring with them a new way of looking at things, a new consciousness. The basic conservatism of the theater troupe is established before the six characters' arrival, in the brief exchange between the Director and actors over Pirandello himself. The Director explains that they are producing *Il Giuòco delle parti (The Rules of the Game)* only because there are no new French comedies available, adding that Pirandello's plays give no pleasure to actors, critics, or audience. Just as Pirandello is mocked by the Director for his new vision of theater, so the new approach to the relationship between art and life offered by the six characters will be scornfully rejected by the conservative theater people.

The separation between the six characters and the acting company is established visually from the beginning. In his description of the six characters at their entrance, Pirandello warns, "anyone who wants to produce this play must use every means possible to make certain that these six characters are not confused with the actors of the company." He suggests the use of a differently colored light at their entrance and even says that masks might be the most effective way of delineating the characters as a separate unit.[7] As for the six characters' costumes, both the material and the cut of the clothing must appear special so that the audience cannot receive the impression that the clothes are "made of a material that could be bought in any shop in the city, or tailored or sewn by any normal dressmaker."

The Director himself frequently refers to the differences between the six characters and the theater company, lest the characters forget that they are the outsiders, dependent on the actors and the Director for their "lives." The Director never adapts to the fact that he is now dealing with characters who challenge his vision of them. He is accustomed to characters who exist only on the printed page and who thus must accept any interpretation the actors and Director thrust upon them, having no argumentative voice of their own. The Director and his actors are outraged at the laughter of the Father and Stepdaughter when they see themselves portrayed by others and challenge the way they are being "interpreted." In fact, the Director, put off balance by the Father's arguments, often tries to fight those arguments by challenging the very "reality" of the characters.

From their entrance the six characters are a disruptive force. They stop the rehearsal and then convince the Director to present their play. In the course of the rehearsal of that play the Father becomes even more threatening. He is presenting a new mode of perception, a vision that suggests that he, as a character, may be more real than the Director and his actors. When the second scene of the characters' play is presented, with the deaths of the two children, the distinguishing line between reality and fiction becomes dangerously unclear. Unable to cope with the uncertainty caused by the characters and their spokesman, the Father, the Director thinks only of the rehearsal time he has lost.

It is not clear from the beginning of the play that the conflict between the Father and the Director will be the play's central one. Although the Father argues passionately to convince the Director that the characters' play should be brought to life, the antagonism between the Father and the Stepdaughter appears to be the most important issue. She insists on revealing their relationship at once, while he tries to soften the impact. As they continue to argue, the facts of the situation are established. The Father had sent his wife away with her lover, who together had thereafter engendered three children. After the lover died, the Mother returned with her children to the town where her husband lived. Her daughter went to work for Madam Pace, whose milliner's shop was also a brothel. The girl was about to act as prostitute for her stepfather when the Mother arrived, revealing the identity of her husband and daughter to each other and preventing the consequences and the encounter from becoming even worse.

The sordidness of this situation, especially for a person of the perceptiveness evinced by the Father throughout the play, would be enough to shame any sensitive man. The Father, however, is a character who has been given only one scene by his creator. His intellectuality, his kindness, and all his other good sentiments and deeds are ignored. His life is summed up in the one action dramatized, an action representative of his carnal weakness as a man. Not only must he be known by just this one action, but he must repeat it in the eternity of art, and be tormented for it by his Stepdaughter, who also knows him only at this one moment.

The Father, the man of intellect trapped in a moment of carnal weakness, articulates his dilemma in a speech early in the play that is one of the central passages not only of this work but of Pirandello's canon:

> The drama for me, signori, is all here, in the consciousness that I have, that we all have and that we believe is a single unit. But that is not true. We have many consciousnesses, signori, as many as the number of possibilities of being that we have in ourselves. We have one for this situation, another for that—and they are very different. But with the illusion intact that we are always the same—"one for all"—and that we are always this one personality in every act we do. It is not true. We become aware of this when, in the midst of one of our acts, by the most wretched of circumstances, we suddenly stop, as if suspended on a hook, and become aware that not all of us is encompassed in that act, and that it would be an atrocious injustice to be judged by that act alone, to be held hooked and suspended there for an entire existence, as if all of our life was summed up in that one act. Now do you understand the wickedness of this girl? She surprised me in a place, in an act, where and how she should not have known me, in a way I should not exist for her, and she wants to give me a reality that I would never have thought to assume for her, in a fleeting, shameful moment of my life. This is what I feel above everything else. . . .

The Father is not trying to escape either the responsibility or the shame of his action, the attempted seduction of his Stepdaughter in Madam Pace's brothel. What he cannot accept, however, is having his entire identity represented by this one act, that he must always wear the mask of sensualist.

The very manner in which the Father states his position helps create the tension Pirandello requires. The Father's argument is presented in a complex structure, couched in carefully constructed rhetoric. He is arguing formally for the multiplicity of the personality and against the injustice of being known by only one facet of it. Despite the theoretical nature of much of what he is saying, his argument is very deeply felt. In order, however, to convince his hearers that he is a reflective man of intellect, he tries to emphasize his thought rather than his emotions. A man of reason has been caught in an act of passion and is now being threatened by constant identification with that act. With his statement, in both its form and its substance, he is trying to refute what his Stepdaughter alleges, that the act of lust at Madam Pace's determines his identity.

Despite the intellectual surface of the Father's argument, his passionate convictions are also communicated. Through the character of the Father we see that the play itself is about the interaction of thought and passion, reason and emotion. Although the Father's intellectuality is manifested through the sophistication of his presentations, it is balanced not only by the picture supplied by the Stepdaughter but also by his own passion in presenting his case to the Director and the actors. The Father is attempting to justify himself and his life, to prove that he is not merely a man of the flesh. His commitment, however, convinces us even more that he is not a pure theoretician, arguing solely because he believes in the rectitude of his formulations.

As we learn more about the Father, it becomes clear that much of his family's crisis was caused by his attempt to deal intellectually with affairs of the heart. He sent his wife away with her lover because he thought it was the best solution to their problem. He could not foresee either his own emotional needs or the disastrous results of his generosity. The suffering of this play has its roots in the best of intentions, in an idea that appeared at first to be fair and compassionate but that ultimately led to great sorrow.

Six Characters encompasses deep suffering along with its theoretical formulations. A discerning audience, faced with the way in which the six characters torture each other while the Father attempts to justify their existence, will become aware of both elements. The bizarre and even at times comic surface of the six characters will yield, through an apprehension of the *sentimento del contrario*, to an appreciation of the agony beneath the surface, particularly the philosophical surface created by the Father. Even though the six characters' suffering is clothed in melodramatic trappings, there is a reality to that suffering that transcends its surface, a reality that Pirandello communicates through the depth of feeling given to his six sufferers. If this reality is rejected because it is melodramatic, then the audience has failed to move to the *sentimento* level.

Despite the depth of these passions, there is one person who refuses to believe in their reality. This figure is the Director, and it is he who remains on the *avvertimento* level throughout the play. He cannot proceed beyond the fact that the characters are literary constructs and thus are not real. Consequently, he not only fails to perceive the Father's suffering but also rejects his ideas. He seems threatened by the intensity of the Father's thoughts and feelings, as well as by the novelty of his ideas; and he runs away from both, seeking refuge in the superficial fact of the characters' unreality. Cast in the unfamiliar role of an audience member, he denies the authenticity of the performance he is forced to witness.

The director's refusal to deal with the depth of the characters' thoughts and feelings is emphasized not only by his own actions, culminating in his final outburst that he has wasted an entire day, but by the contrast that is set up between him and at least some of the members of his company. The actors begin by sharing his skepticism and then echo his growing enthusiasm for the characters' play. They all become antagonistic, however, when the characters want to play themselves and mock the actors' attempts to interpret them, especially in the reenactment of the Father-Stepdaughter scene at Madam Pace's.

Despite the animosity felt by the actors, it is impossible for at least some of them to remain detached. Their interest in the characters is evident throughout. In fact, the characters complain at times that the actors are observing them too closely. The climax of that involvement occurs at the very end of the play, before the entire relationship between the six characters and the theater is shattered. The characters are re-creating the garden scene in which the Little Girl drowns and the Little Boy shoots himself. As soon as the revolver shot is heard, the following dialogue and stage action occur:

THE MOTHER *(with a heartrending scream, running toward her son, with all the actors in the midst of general disorder):* My son! My son! *(And then, amid the confusion and shouting of the other).* Help! Help!

THE DIRECTOR *(also above the shouts, trying to elbow his way through the crowd, while the son is lifted by his head and feet and carried away to a place behind the white curtain):* Is he hurt? Is he hurt? *(Everyone, except the Director and the Father, who have remained near the stairway, on the ground level, will now disappear behind the cyclorama, which has just been lowered, and will remain behind it, speaking with great distress, for a few moments. Then, from both sides of the stage, the actors return to view.)*

THE LEADING LADY *(entering from the right, grieving):* He's dead! The poor boy! He's dead! Oh, what a thing!

THE LEADING MAN *(entering from the left, laughing):* But what do you mean, dead! It's make-believe, pretense. Don't believe it!

OTHER ACTORS FROM THE RIGHT: Make-believe? Reality. Reality! He's dead!

OTHER ACTORS FROM THE LEFT: No! It's make-believe, fiction.

THE FATHER: But what make believe! Reality, reality, signori, reality! *(He disappears behind the backcloth.)*

THE DIRECTOR *(unable to take any more of this):* Make-believe! Reality! Go to the devil all of you. Lights! Lights! Lights! *(Suddenly the entire stage and the auditorium is bathed in very bright light. The Director acts as if he has been liberated from a nightmare, and everyone looks bewildered and as if suspended in space.)* Ah! Nothing like this has ever happened to me. They've made me lose an entire day!

At least part of the acting company has been won over to the six characters' view of their reality. Even those who remain on the Director's side treat the issue as a serious one and do not dismiss it summarily, as he does.

In contrast, the Director's final reaction is shown to be an escape, his attempt to avoid coming to terms with a complex, enigmatic, and painful situation. He purposely does not make contact with either the Father's arguments or the anguish behind those arguments. He has been confronted with a serious issue, the multiplicity of the human personality and the tragedy of being known for only one facet of that personality; instead of trying to make some kind of intellectual or emotional connection, or, best of all, a connection that combines the two, he has sought retreat in the shallow concerns of his work.

The Director's reaction, first to the Father's words, and then to the children's deaths, is crucial. It is only through his explanation of the family's past that the Father can justify their reality, a reality that is in conflict with the appearance of the scenes given them by the playwright who created the characters and then abandoned them. The Father wants to be understood by the Director so that the Director can then help him make the reality of the six characters known to others. It becomes a matter of communication.

While Pirandello is a playwright who allows his characters to theorize about abstract issues, at the same time he dramatizes these ideas in concrete, personal terms. The problem of communication is a perfect example of this combination of the general and the specific. Soon after the arrival of the six characters, the Father and the Stepdaughter both try to present their versions of what has happened between them. The Father asks permission to argue his side, since the girl makes charges without giving out the necessary information:

THE STEPDAUGHTER: This is not the place for narration.

THE FATHER: But I'm not going to narrate. I just want to explain what happened.

THE STEPDAUGHTER: Oh, that's fine. Your version of what happened, of course. *(The Director returns to the stage from the auditorium at this point so that he can restore order.)*

THE FATHER: But this is where all the difficulty lies! In words! We all have inside ourselves a world of things; each one of us has his own world. And how can we possibly understand each other, signori, if in the words I utter I place the sense and value of things as they are inside of me, while to the person listening to me those words inevitably assume the meaning and values they have for him, in the world he inhabits within himself? We think that we understand each other, but we never really do. Take, for example, my pity, all my pity for this woman *(he indicates his wife)* that she interprets as the most ferocious kind of cruelty.

The ideas expressed by the Father not only are fully dramatized throughout the play, in his relationships with the mother, his Stepdaughter and his Son, and perhaps most vividly with the Director and the actors, but also deeply affect him on a personal level, as thoughts whose consequences are felt.

Although the conflict between the Father and the Stepdaughter expresses the difficulty of communication and the differing interpretation of the same phenomenon, the conflict between the Father and the Director becomes the center of this play because it embodies Pirandello's insights into human behavior and the way in which people can attempt to escape from that kind of insight. The Father suffers for his inability to be the man of reason he both wants and believes himself to be. His passions are too strong to allow the retention of this identity, resulting in an action that is the opposite of what his reason would counsel. He must then try to use that reason not only to justify the actions of his "other side" but to convince others that he is more than a sensualist. Yet even as he argues intellectually about the multiplicity and constant change of the personality or the paradox that the six characters are more real than the actors, the suffering behind the theorizing reveals itself.

The Director has very close contact with this complex interpenetration of reason and passion exhibited by the Father. Yet he refuses to accept the reality of the Father's suffering or the insights into the human condition he articulates. This failure to see is caused less by stupidity than by fear, a fear of the new. The Father presents a severe challenge to the notion that man is basically a rational creature who can maintain control over all aspects of himself, including his actions, his personality, and the way he is perceived by others. The Director is not ready to accept this challenge and the uncertainty it suggests, and he flees first into practicality and then out of the theater itself.

The fact that the confrontation between the Father and the Director takes place in a theater is not accidental. The theatrical aspects of this play are neither peripheral nor secondary to the central conflict but are integral parts of it. The characters, in particular the Father and the Stepdaughter, want their story to be enacted on the stage, to be presented for an audience. They seek self-justification and, in the daughter's case, revenge. Their first audience is the company of actors and the Director, and what they present for this ensemble is not an outline or even a script but a performance.

When the six characters first arrive and tell of their abandonment by the playwright, they appear to be searching for an author who will make their story into a play that can then be cast, rehearsed, and performed in the customary theatrical process. It becomes clear, however, that what they are really seeking is a producer, someone who will provide them with the occasion and the proper setting to present their own drama. The characters have not anticipated the theatrical tradition whereby characters themselves never appear on the stage. They are horrified when they see the actors who will be entrusted with portraying them, and they are even more horrified, although also amused, when the actors attempt to re-create the scene in Madam Pace's shop after they have just enacted it.

This scene is the heart of the play, since it dramatizes, in completely theatrical terms, the central issue of interpretation and misinterpretation of a person and his or her actions. Before the actors even begin their version of the scene, there are objections, such as the Stepdaughter's complaint that the actress assuming her role is not dressed in black. As the actors begin, Pirandello notes the following:

The representation of the scene, as executed by the actors, will appear, from the first line, as something entirely different, without ever having, even slightly, the air of a parody. Naturally the Stepdaughter and the Father, unable in fact to recognize themselves in this leading actor or actress who are speaking their very words, express, in various ways, such as gestures, smiles or open protestations, their impressions of surprise, shock, and horror. . . .

The actor's first line as the Father, "Good morning, signorina," brings the reaction, "Oh, no," from the Father. As both the Father and Stepdaughter suggest, the actor's manner and tone of voice are all wrong. He is creating his impression of a man approaching a prostitute, while the Father and Stepdaughter see this action in an entirely different light. Another argument concerns a word which the actor had heard incorrectly when the characters performed the scene. The difficulty of communication and the problems in knowing other people are shown in theatrical terms as the actors attempt to re-create the scene they have just watched; in fact, they are presenting their interpretations and to some extent stereotypes of the characters and their actions.

The Father and Stepdaughter do not recognize themselves in the re-enactment of the actor and actress both because of surface details (a dress of the wrong color, a misheard word) and because the spirit in which the actors present them has been altered. The actors do not have the intense personal involvement with the material the characters have, and this detachment allows them to approach the scene with less "seriousness." The actors are creating what is for them an artificial situation (even though they are trying to give reality to it and thus bring it to life) and are not justifying their own behavior. They are more aware of the surface details of the situation—an older man entering a brothel to meet a prostitute—than the agony of the two characters who find themselves in these circumstances. Throughout this scene, in the clash between what the characters have presented and what the actors are now reenacting, Pirandello dramatizes an excellent example of the difference between the *avvertimento* level (the actors' version) and the *sentimento* level (the characters' version) of reality as articulated in *L'umorismo*.

The scene in Madam Pace's shop also illustrates a more literal use of *umorismo*. The arrival of Madam Pace earlier in the scene and then the actors' version of the characters' encounter are dramatic moments that at first appear comic. Madam Pace speaks a mixture of Italian and Spanish that is comic even to the people onstage, and the Director plans to use her for comic relief. Yet despite her comic aspect, Madam Pace is a sinister figure who uses the Stepdaughter's poverty to employ her, not as a salesgirl in a milliner's shop, but as a prostitute. The arrival of the Mother and her confrontation with Madam Pace, with the concomitant need to separate the two women, further demonstrates the dire circumstances of which Madam Pace is taking advantage, as well as the increased suffering for which she is responsible.

The Madam Pace episode serves as the prelude to the confrontation between the Father and the Stepdaughter and to the distorted reflection of the scene that follows. Just as the seriousness of Madam Pace's actions becomes evident only after we go beyond the superficial comic aspects, so the same is true with the actors' version of the characters' scene. The intensity of emotion between Father and Stepdaughter has been very strong, and at first the more relaxed approach of the actors is welcome, as well as amusing. The response of the characters to the actors' performance, however, signals the cessation of the comedy. It is impossible for the Father and Stepdaughter to find anything amusing in their confrontation, even when it is distorted almost beyond recognition. As the audience watches their reaction and is drawn into empathy for their grief, the fact that these are characters rather than people becomes irrelevant. The misinterpretation and distortion of their suffering, contrasted with the reality of that anguish previously enacted, make the comic response impossible both for the characters themselves and for the sensitive members of the audience.

Pirandello's use of the reversal of the *contrario* goes beyond the comic in this play. One of the most important of these contrasts occurs in the seeming paradox that the characters are more real than the actors. Since the characters are fictional constructs, whereas the actors are "real people," the assumption would be that the actors would be able to give life to the characters. The exact opposite occurs. The life the characters create in their confrontations is drained from them when the actors take over. The actors present a shadow of what the characters' reality is. The audience, by seeing the characters first and then the actors, has this clearly demonstrated for them, even before the Father articulates the position later in the play.

The Father argues that the characters are more "real" than the actors because of the fixity of their personalities. While "real people" are constantly changing, like actors assuming different roles and characteristics, as they age or find themselves in new situations, the characters are stable, having been created in one way by their author. The agony of their necessity to repeat the same actions over and over has been shown previously. The Father's point here, however, is that as painful as this fixity is, it gives the characters a reality that the human beings who change from one moment to the next do not possess. Once again Pandello has not merely suggested this idea theoretically but has dramatized it in theatrical terms and made it part of the emotional reality of the character who articulates it.

The reality of the characters is also reinforced by the appearance of Madam Pace. Although she belongs to the world of the characters, she does not travel with them because she is not a member of the family and thus cannot remain with the Mother, who blames her for the Family's dilemma. When Madam Pace is needed for the crucial scene, however, she appears. She is part of the theatrical reality of the six characters, and since this reality is fixed, her presence can be summoned by their evocation. After she performs her necessary service, she disappears again, having left the immediate consciousness of the characters whose reality determines her own.

As early as 1904 Pirandello described the independence of his characters, how they put him to work at their service, when he wrote to Luigi Natoli:

> if material cares and social duties didn't distract me, I believe that I could spend from morning to evening at my desk, serving the characters of my narratives, who are crowded within me. Each wants to assume life before the others. They all have a particular misery they want revealed. I sympathize with them.[8]

In 1911, ten years before *Six Characters,* he wrote a story, "The Tragedy of a Character," where as narrator he speaks of being visited by two to three characters per week. Then, in the preface to *Six Characters,* he continues the same line, insisting that once an author creates characters, he can do nothing to deny their existence.

There are indications, moreover, that Pirandello was not merely employing a literary conceit appropriate to his artistic vision when he wrote in these terms. According to his daughter, Lietta:

> he was a blazing furnace, as if an entire secret world existed within him, clamoring to be revealed. His mind never rested. He was always looking within, as if he were trying to discover a deeper reality beneath surface appearances. He would discuss his characters with us as if they were real people, more real than those who were alive. Bit by bit he would read what he was writing to myself, my brothers and close friends who gathered at our home. His absorption was so fierce and compelling that often we were not only disturbed but overwhelmed.[9]

In the same vein, a French critic, Alfred Mortier, after a long, private interview with Pirandello held in 1924, concluded that the Italian author was possessed and haunted by his characters, who ended up putting the pen in his hand and constraining him to write, dictating to him what their passions suggested. Thus, the characters inhabited his brain but led a real, insistent, hallucinatory existence outside him at the same time.[10]

In both *That's the Way Things Are* and *Six Characters* Pirandello posits the necessity of being open to new modes of perception. In *That's the Way Things Are* his ideas are presented within a basically realistic framework. In *Six Characters* the veristic illusion is shattered to use the machinery of the theater for the dramatization of a new approach to reality. Pirandello's theater is a mirror that creates a crisis in a man's life by reflecting to him a vision of himself. The Father reacts to the crisis of seeing himself distorted, first in the account of his life given by the Stepdaughter, and then in the actors' interpretation of his scene. He comes into open conflict with the Director over the conception of the characters' drama as well as the relative reality of the different modes of existence to which the two men belong.

The suffering of the six characters, as well as the concept of the constant change of the human personality articulated by the Father, also constitutes a crisis for the Director. This crisis is, to a large extent, a theatrical one, since he has been an audience member to the drama presented by the characters. By analogy, then, Pirandello is demonstrating to his audience in the theater that refusal to come to terms with the interaction of intellect and emotion in the Father, as well as the ideas of the fragmentation of consciousness and mutability of personality he propounds, is the same kind of escapism as practiced by the Director, who must flee from anything that threatens his own vision of reality.

In presenting the idea that the characters may have a greater reality than the actors, the supposedly real people of the play, Pirandello is actually justifying the necessity of art. The aesthetic experience, by means of its selectivity and crystallization of images, communicates to people in ways that events in life cannot. There is a sense of constant change in life that cannot be captured in the permanence of art. Yet that very motion and change, so venerated by Filippo Marinetti and the Futurists, for example, make it difficult to formulate significant perceptions about life. It is the artist who captures his audience in certain poses and then confronts it with his images. Thus, Pirandello's work never exists for its own sake, as does the aestheticism of D'Annunzio, but serves to reveal to the members of his audience what they look like beneath the facades and ever shifting self-projections they have created for themselves.

The crisis for the audience is created both by the disturbing ideas that are being dramatized and by the way in which they are presented. Pirandello has changed the shape of the mirror so that it looks more like a mirror than it has before. The reaction of the opening-night audience shows that Pirandello was right in anticipating that the novelty of his insistence on the reality of the theater itself would precipitate a crisis for his audience. Those who dismissed his experiment out of hand are thus mirroring the Director and falling into the trap that has been set for them, proving the validity of the play's content by overreacting to its formulistic experimentation.

It must be carefully acknowledged that Pirandello is playing a game here. He has not substituted the total unstructured reality of the theater for the old-fashioned play. He has written a play, and while there are small moments that allow for improvisation, he is still in control of what he is communicating. What he is changing, therefore, is the type of theatrical illusion being created, substituting an illusion that is one step closer to "the truth" than the old illusions. Although a good production of this play may convince some members of the audience that they are really watching a rehearsal interrupted by a group of outsiders, this illusion can last only for a certain time. In fact, it becomes just one of the many appearances that are shattered before the play is completed.

Pirandello's genius can be discerned in the skill with which he manipulates the theatrical formulation of his ideas. Just when the audience has settled into an acceptance of his play as theatrical illusion, he challenges this assumption by a stunning coup de theatre. The suicide of the little boy, announced to the actors and characters and to the audience by a gunshot, once more plunges the proceedings into chaos, highlighted by charges and countercharges of "pretense" and "reality." As Richard Gilman so eloquently writes, "To anyone not deadened by the kind of scholarship that converts artistic phenomenon into cultural data, to hear this shot during a performance of *Six Characters*—no matter how bad the production or how often one has seen or read the play—is to have one's ideas about drama changed in an instant or an earlier change reconfirmed." [11]

Almost everything in Pirandello's best plays is something more or less than what it originally appears to be. He insists on this complexity, both in the subject matter and in the formulation of his works. This complexity can have its playful side as well as its more serious aspect, as seen in the use of his own previous play *The Rules of the Game* as the original script in rehearsal at the start of *Six Characters*. In the explanation the Director gives of the egg the Leading Actor must use as a prop, Pirandello in fact mocks what audiences and critics have found in his plays by giving the kind of elaborate, purely intellectual symbolic analysis that captures some of the surface but little of the essence of his dramaturgy.

The Director identifies the empty eggshell as the "empty form of reason, without the filling of instinct, which is blind." He then proceeds to identify the husband of the play as the representative of reason, and the wife of instinct, a statement that has more validity than the blatant symbolic interpretation of the egg. The acting troupe, led by the Director, does not want to do Pirandello's play, however, since they do not understand his complexity and think that such obvious intellectualizations are the essence of his work. Even before he has introduced his six characters, Pirandello has prepared the way for their ultimate rejection, both by the Director and by those in the audience who share his insistence on remaining on the surface so that their basic assumptions will not be challenged.

Although I have spoken of the Director's statement about losing a day of rehearsal as if it were the end of the play, there is a final stunning theatrical image that Pirandello added in the second edition of his play, one that sums up what has gone before in strikingly visual terms.[12] After the Director has spoken of the lost time, he dismisses the actors until the evening and tells the electrician to turn off all the lights. The request is granted, and in total darkness the Director says, "For God's sake, at least leave me a light so I can find my way out of here." At this point, from behind the cyclorama, comes a green light projecting the giant shadows of the characters, minus the two young children who are dead. Upon seeing this image the Director runs from the stage and out the auditorium, terrified by the vision he has just seen. The light behind the cyclorama goes out, and the characters emerge from behind it onto the stage. The Stepdaughter then flees from the remaining three characters, also running through the auditorium and laughing wildly as she runs.

The Director's inability to be free of the characters as easily as he would like suggests the firmness of the reality they have established. Both as abstract representatives of the literary aspects of theater and as concrete embodiments, they have communicated their thoughts and emotions so strongly that they have established their right to occupy the stage. The Director flees because he is unwilling, and/or unable, to make the imaginative leap to accept the authenticity of their reality. To work in the theater requires a belief in its phantasms as well as its more obvious realities, like scenery, costume, and makeup. Since the Director cannot move beyond the *avvertimento* surface level of their existence as "characters" rather than as people, he deserves the fright the characters accord him.

The flight of the Stepdaughter serves as counterpoint to that of the Director. She is rebelling against the vision of reality presented by the Father, who acts as the spokesman, not for Pirandello, but for the six characters. She interprets his actions and those of the other members of the family in an entirely different way. Yet she is a part of that reality, even when she makes her exodus. She is acting out the final moment of the characters' drama when she leaves. First the two young children are killed, and then the Stepdaughter leaves, so that the three characters who remain constitute the family that existed before the Father sent his wife away with her lover. The Stepdaughter challenges the interpretation of the Father's reality rather than its existence, so that her departure, even in cynical laughter, participates in that reality, while the Director tries but fails to deny it.

Pirandello's *umorismo*, the advocacy of a new way of seeing that penetrates beneath the surface to the emotional reality underneath, finds its formulation in theatrical terms in *Six Characters*. The actors and Director should understand the strange predicament of the six characters better than anyone else, since they deal in phantasms, interpretation, and that strange middle ground that combines illusion and reality. Yet the theater people betray their theatrical trust because they refuse to probe beyond the surfaces and are not open to the new relationship offered by the characters, a relationship that is more intensely personal than the one with the scripts they are accustomed to dealing with.

The three characters who have taken the stage at the end of the play have not found their playwright but have discovered that they do not really need him as much as they need an audience and a theater. The two scenes he has written for them are the crux of their drama, and the rest of their background is known to, and can be articulated by, them. They have also discovered the difficulty of knowing and interpreting the human personality, whether it be of a person or his shadow, the character. This difficulty is compounded when the other person is unwilling to make the effort to understand the essence of one's reality, in this case the suffering that exists despite the fictitious origin of their existence. It is the strength of this reality, despite its illusionary appearance, that allows the characters to occupy the stage at the end of the play.[13]

As the Father had said earlier, "When a character is born, he immediately acquires an independence from even his author that is so great that he can be imagined in other situations in which the author had not thought of placing him, and even acquire, at times, a significance that the author had not dreamed of giving to him." It is this independence that has led the six characters into the theater and their confrontation with the Director and his company. Yet one of the paradoxes of the play reveals that while there may be such independence from the author, in the theater there is no such freedom from the actors, the director, and the audience.

The theater presents its characters only through the interpretive mirror of those actors and their director. The analogy to nontheatrical life is clear. A person acts on his own, according to his own motives and with a certain vision of those actions and their desired effects in his mind. Yet those actions are subject to the interpretation of his audience, the society with which he must deal, and may be given an interpretation or significance that is not intended by the person originating the act.

Beyond the analogy to everyday life, which the theater often makes, Pirandello is also implying a self-conscious reference to his own personal dilemma. His wife's obsessive jealousy became increasingly pathological. At first she was jealous of her husband's students and would spy on him from outside the gates of the Magistero, where he taught. To avoid any pretext for her suspicions, Pirandello regulated his schedule scrupulously and entrusted financial matters to her care, counting out the money for his tram ride, newspapers, and cigars each day before he left for classes.[14] Antonietta became more, not less, paranoid, however, convinced that Pirandello and their daughter had forged an alliance against her. She forced Lietta to taste their food before she would eat it and, after making veiled suggestions, one day accused the daughter of an incestuous relationship with her father. The horrified girl tried to shoot herself with an old revolver that fortunately no longer worked, but she had to be sent to live with an aunt in Florence, leaving Pirandello alone in the house with his deluded wife.[15]

Pirandello's predicament is thus similar to the Father's, who is trying to convince the Stepdaughter and the actors of his true nature. No matter what Pirandello did or said to convince his wife of his fidelity, she would not alter her interpretation of his character. From time to time Pirandello would suggest that Lietta be permitted to return home, but Antonietta insisted that only one of them could live under his roof. Like the Father, he was given the false identity of libertine and sensualist by a woman who saw him in a completely opposite way from his own self-identification. Thus, *Six Characters*, written less than two years after Antonietta finally had to be confined in a private clinic, arises neither from abstruse intellectualization nor from melodramatic imagining but from the "unreal" reality of life itself.

Six Characters also dramatizes Pirandello's professional dilemma. As an artist, the theater is the perfect medium for the communication of his particular vision. But by using the theater he renders himself dependent on actors and a director who will then interpret his words and ideas. Furthermore, he is also at the mercy of his audience, who may very well either not comprehend or be hostile to what he considers to be the essence of his work. This idea is merely suggested here; in the second play of the trilogy, *Each in His Own Way*, it will become one of the central issues raised.

As the characters stand on the theater stage, supplanting the actors who were called upon to bring them to life and failed, the ambiguous nature of the theatrical experience is given a final image. Those people who have failed to apprehend humoristically the suffering beneath the intellectual surface have departed, even those who should have been most sympathetic to the dilemma of characters dependent on them for their life. Communication, especially the communication of suffering that will elicit a compassionate response, has failed both on a theatrical level (the actors' interpretations of the characters' suffering) and on a nontheatrical level (the dismissal of the reality of that suffering by the Director and part of his company).

All that remains now is the characters and the audience. If any communication has been made, it must be between these two groups, so that the audience has been brought to an awareness of the facts and a sympathetic understanding of their significance. If this has been accomplished and Pirandello's *umorismo* has worked, then the audience will leave the theater with the insight that the creatures of make-believe, the characters, have been given a reality of suffering that makes them the most real figures in the play, the ones who have the most to communicate to us about ourselves and the human condition.

4.

Each in His Own Way (1924)

As is often the case with prophets or innovators in an artistic form, recognition and appreciation of what Pirandello had accomplished in *Six Characters in Search of an Author* occurred first not in his native Italy but in Paris, the center of the artistic avant-garde during this period. Great acclaim greeted the French premiere of *Six Characters* directed by Georges Pitoëff in 1923. Although Pirandello had some disagreements with Pitoëff over his approach to the play (including the use of an elevator at the rear of the stage for the first appearance of the six characters), he owed much of his international reputation to the French, and especially Pitoëff's productions of *Six Characters* and subsequent works.[1]

When he came to the writing of the second play in his theater trilogy, *Each in His Own Way, (Ciascuno a suo modo)*, it appears that Pirandello was more conscious of his domestic failure than of his international success. For this play he chose a different technique from that of the theater plays that precede and follow it. In both *Six Characters* and *Tonight We Improvise* the theatrical nature of the work is acknowledged from the outset. Both plays are peopled with actors, directors, characters, and other theatrical personnel who are involved in the creation of a production, either in rehearsal *(Six Characters)*, or in improvised performance *(Tonight We Improvise)*. The audience is aware from the start that the playwright has abandoned the customary mode of verisimiltude for a more precise realism that does not try to ignore the basic nature of the theatrical experience.

Each in His Own Way, on the other hand, does not make its theatrical nature known from the beginning. The curtain rises on a drawing room, creating the expectation that Pirandello has written a more traditional play than his preceding theatrical experiment. As the first act unfolds and the central characters and issues are presented, the impression that this is a veristic play, at least in the use of setting, plot, and character, is reinforced. As the curtain is brought down on the close of the first act, nothing has suggested that this play has a closer kinship to *Six Characters* than to *That's the Way Things Are* or the even more solidly realistic *Vestire gli ignudi (To Clothe the Naked)*. A situation has been introduced, different interpretations of that situation presented, and the groundwork for a typically Pirandellian play about conflicting versions of "the truth" has been laid.

The first-act curtain does not signal the customary pause; it is immediately raised again to reveal a new setting, that of the lobby of the theater where the play is being presented. The theater stage now mirrors part of the theater itself, and the actors on that stage mirror members of that audience. This scene, labeled a choral interlude, then unfolds as a series of comments on what has just transpired in the first act. That act as we have just watched it is now identified as a theatrical fiction. Although this is not startling information, its acknowledgment on the stage where it has been presented does generate surprise. We are meant to see these events and characters, not as real unto themselves, but as creations of the playwright Pirandello.

The structure of *Each in His Own Way* creates a tension between the play being presented and the fictitious audience's response to it, both of which are viewed by the real audience. Two acts of the play are shown, each followed by a choral interlude that comments on, and analyzes, what has just occurred. Two fictions are thus created: one mirrors life outside the theater; the other mirrors the theater itself and the reaction of people in that theater to the fiction they have just seen. Since Pirandello's plays usually elicted a violent response, he is anticipating the reaction of the real audience by showing it to them before they have the opportunity to articulate it themselves.

Although the dramatization of the audience reaction to what can be called a quintessential Pirandello play might be a sufficient theatrical device to show the variety of violently clashing responses to the same phenomenon and the predictability of those responses, Pirandello is interested in an even more important issue. To explore this question, he adds what he himself identifies as a third level, a level beyond those of the play itself and its audience. This third level is created by making the Delia Morello–Michele Rocca story being shown on stage into a *commedia a chiave,* a play with a key (i.e., a play based on supposedly real persons and events).[2] Beyond the issues raised by the play itself and the audience reaction to it, Pirandello is concerned with the amount of truth a playwright can reflect in his theatrical mirror before the people who see themselves in that mirror move to smash it.

Although the existence of real-life models for the characters of his play and the presence of those people in the audience are revealed after the other two levels, Pirandello has set the groundwork for his *commedia a chiave* before the real audience has even entered the auditorium. *Six Characters* represented Pirandello's break with the limits of the proscenium arch. In *Each in His Own Way* he extends the domain of that cleavage even further, to the street outside the theater and to the lobby where tickets are being sold and people are gathering as they prepare to enter the theater. Even before the play itself begins, the audience is being readied for the type of theatrical event they will experience.

As I suggested in chapter III, Pirandello gives brief portions of *Six Characters* an improvisatory quality to establish a sense of the real life of actors in rehearsal. Here he provides a two-page scenario, including the text of a flyer to be given to audience members before they enter the theater. This scenario, omitted in the Arthur Livingston English version,[3] sets up the *commedia a chiave* and makes the later events more easily comprehensible. Since this prologue not only prepares the audience for the most important level of the play but also represents Pirandello's attempt to extend the bounds of his theater even further, I will quote the complete text:[4]

The performance of this play should begin on the street, or more properly, in the plaza in front of the theater, with the announcement (shouted by two or three newsboys) and sale of an "evening newspaper," properly printed on a flyer, done so that it would appear as a special edition. On this page, in bold letters and easily seen, in the middle, would be inserted the following indiscretion, in typical journalistic style:

THE SUICIDE OF THE SCULPTOR LA VELA AND THIS EVENING'S PLAY AT THE THEATRE....
(the name of the theater)

In the theater world there has suddenly arisen a situation destined to stir up an enormous scandal. It seems that Pirandello has taken the argument of his new play *Each in His Own Way,* which will be premiered tonight at the ———Theater from the dramatic suicide of the young sculptor Giacomo La Vela that occurred a few months ago in Torino. It will be remembered that La Vela, having surprised the noted actress A. M., his fiancée, in intimate intercourse with Baron N. in his studio on Via Montevideo, instead of taking action against the two culprits, turned on himself and committed suicide.

It also seems that Baron N. was engaged to one of La Vela's sisters. The impression produced by the tragic event remains vivid, not only because of the fame the young sculptor had already achieved, but also because of the social position and the notoriety of the others involved in the tragedy. It is very probable that some unpleasant incident may occur tonight in the theater.

This is not enough. The spectators who enter the theater to buy tickets will see, in the area around the ticket office, the actress of whom the newspaper article gave the initials A. M., that is, Amelia Moreno, there in person, with three gentlemen in smoking jackets who are trying in vain to convince her to give up her intention of attending the performance of the play. They want to take her away: they implore her to be good and at least let them remove her from a position where she can be seen by so many people who might recognize her. Does she want a scandal? Why doesn't she allow them to take her somewhere else? But she refuses. Even though she is pale and upset, she wants to stay, to see the play, at least until that arrogant playwright arrives. She puts a handkerchief to her face and then tears it away as soon as she is aware that someone is noticing her, and either hides herself or rails at them. She repeats to her friends that she wants a box in the third tier: she will stand in the rear so that she won't be seen. She bids them to go and buy the tickets. She promises that she won't cause a scandal, that she will leave if she cannot stand it. A third tier box—do they want her to buy it herself?

This improvised scene, played as if it were true, must begin a few minutes before the time set for the beginning of the play and must last, amid the surprise, the curiosity and perhaps even some apprehension of the spectators, up until the bell is rung signaling the raising of the curtain.

Meanwhile, concurrently, the spectators already in the theater, or those entering, will find in the theater lobby, or perhaps in the corridor outside the auditorium, another surprise, another source of curiosity and perhaps apprehension, in another scene, this one between Baron Nuti and his friends.

"Take it easy, take it easy: I am calm, cannot you see? Very calm. And I assure you that I will be even calmer if you go away. You're attracting everyone's attention, massed around me as you are. Leave me alone and no one will pay any attention to me. After all, I'm just a member of the audience, like everyone else. What can I do, in a theater? I know that she will come, if she hasn't arrived already. I want to see her again, but just see her, from a distance. I don't want anything else, I assure you. Now will you leave? Don't make a show for these people who come to amuse themselves at my expense. How can I convince you that I want to be by myself. I am very calm—can I be more calm than this?"

He will continue, back and forth, with his face troubled and his body shaking, until all the spectators are seated in the theater.

All this might explain to the audience why the theater management thought it wise to note the following in the program: *Nota Bene*. It is not possible to give the precise number of acts of this play. There will be two or three, depending on the likely incidents that might keep the performance from being completed.

This scenario presents a great challenge to the director of the play, especially for all performances after the premiere. The difficulty of making the improvised scenes both convincing and accessible to the incoming audience is exacerbated by both the novelty of the material and the strangeness of the milieu in which it is to be performed. The use of the handbill and these improvised scenes featuring the actress and the baron are not capricious, however. In this play Pirandello attempts perhaps his boldest experiment in the juxtaposition of the intellectual and emotional sides of life, as well as life outside the theater with that on the stage. This juxtaposition is developed in all three levels of the play, but reaches its culmination in the third level, the *commedia a chiavé* relationship between Amelia Moreno and Baron Nuti and their mirror images on the stage, Delia Morello and Michele Rocca.

The audience entering the theater might be puzzled and perhaps amused by the handbill and the lobby scenes, but will probably put them out of mind as the first act and then the first choral interlude are presented. When the *commedia a chiave* is finally introduced as the third level of the play, however, they will have some reference point, some suggestion that the world inside the theater and the world outside are interacting in some strange and novel way. Since *Each in His Own Way* is a play that ends in disruption and chaos, it is appropriate that it also begin in confusion. The improvisatory scenes thus prepare the audience for the atmosphere and give them the background for the events of the play they will shortly see.

As Pirandello premiered his plays, he was faced with a critical barrage attacking his extremism and his intellectuality. In this play he seems intent on defending the true nature of his work against this argument in the most complex way possible. After the prologue has been completed, the curtain rises on a first act that seems to be the quintessence, but is really a parody, of what has often been thought of as "Pirandellianismo." The first act offers a Pirandello play, not as conceived by its author, but as perceived by at least part of his audience. In exploring the distortions that can accompany perception and interpretation, Pirandello daringly offers a mirror image of what he has written previously, choosing to dramatize the vision of his work projected by his critics and detractors.

As *Each in His Own Way* begins, the opening conversation, between two men identified only as the Slender Young Man and the Old Man, is another prologue, this time to the "play within the play." The conversation establishes absolutely nothing about the play we are about to see, but it does set the mood and, more important, tells us that we are in Pirandello country. These two characters do not figure in the rest of the play and are clearly placed here in order to mock what people have previously identified as abstruse philosophizing:

THE SLENDER YOUNG MAN: But what do you think?
THE OLD MAN: What do I think! *(pause)*. I wouldn't know *(pause)*. What do the others think about it?
THE SLENDER YOUNG MAN: Oh! Some say one thing, some another.
THE OLD MAN: Of course. Each has his own opinion.
THE SLENDER YOUNG MAN: But no one, to tell the truth, seems to be sure, it's as if everyone wants to know what the others are saying before they reveal their own opinion.
THE OLD MAN: For my part I am most secure in my opinion, but certainly prudence counsels me to find out if the others know anything that I don't know which might make me modify my opinion.
THE SLENDER YOUNG MAN: But what do you know about it?
THE OLD MAN: Dear friend, we never know everything.
THE SLENDER YOUNG MAN: But what does that do to opinions?
THE OLD MAN: Good God, I hold my opinion ... until someone offers proof to the contrary.
THE SLENDER YOUNG MAN: No, excuse me, but with the admission that we never can know everything, how can you presuppose that such contrary proofs exist?
THE OLD MAN: And by this reasoning you want to conclude that I have no opinion?
THE SLENDER YOUNG MAN: Because according to what you said, no one can ever have any.
THE OLD MAN: And does not this seem to be an opinion?
THE SLENDER YOUNG MAN: Yes, but a negative one.

THE OLD MAN: It is better than nothing, is it not? It is better than nothing, my friend.

After this totally abstract conversation and one between two young women that is only slightly more specific, Pirandello introduces the plot of his play. At a gathering the night before, two men, Doro Palegari and Francesco Savio, have taken opposite sides regarding the guilt or innocence of a woman, Delia Morello. Signorina Morello had been engaged to a young painter, Giorgio Salvi, who discovered her with his sister's prospective husband, Michele Rocca, and committed suicide. Palegari has argued that Signorina Morello is guiltless in her fiancé's death, since she was motivated by a wish to save Salvi from a disastrous liaison, and not by a desire to punish and destroy him, as Savio contends.

When Savio arrives the next morning to inform Palegari that he has reconsidered his position and has been won over by Palegari's arguments, he learns that Palegari has also changed his mind and is now convinced of La Morello's guilt. Each thinks that the other is mocking him, and their quarrel becomes even more bitter than it had been the night before. Moreover, when the one person arrives who should be able to clear up the situation, Delia Morello herself, she does not understand the reasons for her own actions. She wants to believe the argument advanced first by Palegari and then Savio, but cannot be sure that her actions were truly motivated by such altruism.

As I have suggested, the first level of *Each in His Own Way* contains Pirandello's attempt to write the kind of play his critics accused him of writing: elliptical, confused, philosophic. To reinforce this impression, throughout the play within a play Diego Cinci, a friend of Doro Palegari's and an outsider in the controversy involving Palegari; Savio; Delia Morello; and later her lover, Michele Rocca, offers philosophic speeches on the desirability but impossibility of achieving consistency in one's personality. He emphasizes the constant change of the personality and at one point identifies himself as a revolutionary who rejoices in the overthrow of fictitious forms that trap the flow of life.

Besides introducing what might be called an archetypical Pirandellian situation, the first act thus presents a character who appears on the surface to be the perfect stereotype of the Pirandellian *raisonneur* spokesman. Although neither Laudisi nor the Father really served that function, they had been identified as such by contemporary audiences and press. Now Pirandello apparently is providing what his audience claimed he had been giving them all along. Instead of introducing some false clues into his main story, Pirandello creates an entire plot and set of characters that are primarily misleading. The stage audience is taken in, as is the real audience in the auditorium, at least until the use of the *commedia a chiave* is made clear. To most observers this play appears to be focused entirely on an intellectual question. The anguish of Delia Morello's uncertainty over her guilt or innocence is present, but it has been converted into an elaborate puzzle by everyone on stage, including Delia herself: "What was her true motivation?" If we look to the *raisonneur,* Diego Cinci, for clarification, we will only become caught in another of Pirandello's traps.

Pirandello has taken the dialectical analysis articulated in *L'umorismo* and codified by the critic Tilgher, in which the basic conflict in life is between the restrictions of certain fictions or forms and the freedom of the "life force," and has given it to one of his characters, a character designed to appear, superficially, as the figure who dispenses the play's truths. He is not fully integrated into the plot of the play within a play, not because of faulty playwriting, but because Pirandello's technique here is to write in the style that others have assigned to him, creating a surface level of his play that can ultimately be dismissed. While it is true that some of Pirandello's later plays may take the Tilgherian dichotomy too seriously and use it in an undigested form, as Gaspar Giudice argues, in this play Pirandello is misleading those people who categorize his ideas in this way to show them that his work is too complex to be reduced to a formula.

Although Doro Palegari and Francesco Savio are the participants in the argument that dominates the first level of *Each in His Own Way,* and Delia Morello and Michele Rocca the subjects, it is the *raisonneur* figure, Diego Cinci, who seems to be the play's central figure. He is asked to intervene in the controversy by Doro's mother and, even more important, is always on the scene when an important discussion occurs. Of all the characters in the play, he is the one who seems to know the most and to have thought most deeply about the problems of existence that appear to be involved. He also may be anticipating the same kind of ambiguous ending as

That's the Way Things Are, since he does not believe that the mysteries of the human personality can be fathomed.

Pirandello works very carefully to convince his audience that Diego Cinci is an important part of his play. The philosophical positions he articulates are part of the creation of this surface. Since by this point in his career Pirandello has been firmly identified as an abstruse, intellectual writer by at least a portion of his public, this character, who seems to be pointedly articulating the author's "philosophy," must therefore be crucial to the comprehension of the play. Diego's speeches, in which he uses such images as moments of tempest that cause "the destruction of all the fictitious forms by which one's stupid daily life is coagulated," serve to reinforce the appearance that he is the key to unlocking the secret of what is transpiring onstage.

Another important element in this surface level is the sense of mystery with which Diego is invested. The best example of this is a speech early in the play, when Diego is discussing the Delia Morello affair with Doro Palegari's mother, Donna Livia. Diego seems to absent himself from that discussion and begins a reverie about the night his mother died. As he sat by her deathbed he had become fascinated by a fly that had fallen into a glass of water and by the fly's furious attempts to escape. As he watched that fly die, he had not been paying attention to the death of his mother. Donna Livia is thoroughly confused by his motivation in recounting the incident, and she even laughs out of discomfort. Diego of course cannot laugh, since the story haunts him.

Although this small episode seems to have great significance for *Each in His Own Way,* telling us something about the strange way in which the memory works and the different effect the same story can have on different people, I think it is yet another false clue introduced to create a surface reality that will later be contradicted. The real audience is being prepared for a play in which Diego Cinci will be the central figure. He will interpret the actions of the other characters and guide the audience reaction to them. Even though Laudisi did not actually function in this way, he was credited with this role by the critics. Now Pirandello is presenting a man who appears even more blatantly to be that kind of spokesman, an intellectual who will embody the thought content that the playwright wishes to impart to his audience.

If in the plot of *Each in His Own Way* Pirandello parodies himself—or the vision of his playwriting he does not recognize but others assign him (the "many Pirandellos" of the letter to Vittorini)—then he parodies his audience and critics in the choral interlude. He has presented Act I of a play that follows the definition of his dramatic practice accepted by much of the Italian theatergoing public. Now he demonstrates not only how this public would react to such a play but also how they have been responding to their vision of his work in general. Pirandello is coming to terms with his critical and public image here because he sees in it a perfect metaphor for one of the ideas he is trying to communicate in his plays: the problem of perception in interpreting people and events, with conflicting opinions formulated about the same phenomenon.

In dramatizing the response to what they have just seen, Pirandello gives the critics not only differing shades of opinion but diametrically opposite views. In the first choral interlude, one group of critics attacks him as a negativist, while his supporters counterattack with the same accusation against the critics. There are also arguments over the presence or lack of both controversy and poetry in the play. This scene, along with the choral interlude following the second act, becomes a mirror image that reflects both what has just occurred on the stage, a clash of interpretations of the same event, and what would be occurring among the critics and audience members if Pirandello had allowed them their customary pause after Act I. It is quite possible, moreover, that he is anticipating the conversations of the real audience when it is finally allowed to discuss the play. The theatrical mirror is thus reflecting past, present, and future events simultaneously.

One of the critics who takes part in the conversation of the choral interlude states that he wants to reserve judgment. For him attendance at the play has been like watching flashes of lightning. He then adds, "Why, I have the impression that I am looking into a mirror gone crazy." This definition of Pirandello's practices, especially in the theater trilogy, is a particularly apt one. The mirror of the stage is reflecting what goes on inside as well as outside the theater. The mirror of this play is also reflecting the image the public has assigned to Pirandello. This image is seen both in the first act of the play within a play and in the choral interlude that presents audience reaction to that play. Furthermore both the play and the stage audience's response to it reflect the ideas about interpretation and multiplicity that Pirandello is not only dramatizing but proving by the very way in which his dramatic exploration of those subjects is received.[5]

In the notes for his production of *Each in His Own Way*, Luigi Squarzina discusses the many facets he finds in this play.[6] One of the ideas that fascinates him most is the suggestion that since the "play" is supposed to be the premiere of a Pirandello work, the author would be expected to be in the audience. His presence adds another level to the play for both the stage and the real audiences. For the stage audience there is the possibility that the object of the most vehement critics' scorn could pass by at any moment. For the real audience there is the thought that since Pirandello has injected himself so strongly into the play already, he might actually appear to further whatever he is trying to accomplish. When the *commedia a chiave* level is introduced, the possibility of a confrontation between the playwright and the models for his work creates an electricity that could be shared, in different ways, by both audiences.

Pirandello infuses himself into all three of the theater trilogy plays, but only to a minor degree in *Six Characters* and *Tonight We Improvise*. In this play, however, his presence, be it actual or merely suggested, is much more important, since the interpretation of his work by the critics is one of the ways he establishes the themes of diversity of perception and multiplicity of response to the same phenomenon. Act I of the play within a play is a crazy-mirror image of Pirandello's previous work, while the choral response to it illustrates how his plays have been subjected to the same differences in perceptions as have the actions of Delia Morello. Pirandello's audience had made him a prime issue in the evaluation of his work. Now he turns the tables on them, using their responses in an attempt to correct the distortions he found in the image they have assigned to him.

At the end of the first choral interlude, after the play within a play and the stage audience's response to that play have been firmly established, Pirandello returns to the *commedia a chiave* aspect of *Each in His Own Way*. Although he has anticipated its existence with the special edition of the newspaper and the scenes played at the ticket window and in the lobby, he must wait until the audience is introduced to the Delia Morello–Michele Rocca plot and then sees a stage audience react to it as a play before he can actually present the reactions of La Moreno and Baron Nuti to the mirror images they have just seen. Once the existence of this "real-life" basis of the play is reintroduced, however, it substantially colors the real audience's perception of both the play itself and the stage audience's reaction to it. The superficial view of the play as an elaborate Pirandellian charade is now revealed as incomplete.

For two members of the audience, *Each in His Own Way* is not an intellectual exercise but a reflection of their lives. This makes the response of the stage audience and the part of the real audience it mirrors or anticipates inadequate. The *commedia a chiave* level of this play thus becomes its heart, both for the influence it exerts toward the disruption of the play within a play and for the metaphoric reverberations it sends forth. In terms of the crazy-mirror image Pirandello uses, the *commedia a chiave* is the ultimate reflection, real people seeing their actions represented on stage. The knowledge of this "reality" also influences the responses of both audiences. What at first may seem either overintellectual or too melodramatic, or paradoxically a combination of both, takes on new dimensions when it is seen as the reflection of "reality" rather than a fiction. Pirandello uses the same pattern he introduced in *L'umorismo* and then employed in his earlier plays, although with more fragmentation and complexity. A situation is established, a response elicited, and then more information is supplied to necessitate the alteration of that initial reaction.

At the close of the first choral interlude, the news is disseminated among the critics and audience that Amelia Moreno and Baron Nuti are present. Nuti speaks with members of the stage audience, and when they return for the second-act curtain, La Moreno enters with her entourage. She wants to go backstage but decides to return to her seat when she is informed that the second act has begun. Pirandello is introducing the *commedia a chiave* gradually, and it is only at the close of the second act of the play within a play that it will explode and engulf the other two groups—those presenting the play and those watching it.

The second act of the play within a play continues the foolish argument between Palegari and Savio, who are now intent on defending their honor in a duel. The key action occurs, however, when Delia Morello and Michele Rocca both arrive at Savio's house in order to defend themselves against the accusations made against them. They deny their love for each other, and thus any guilt in the suicide of the painter, until they realize that their hatred actually is a mask for love. The act ends as they leave the Savio house together, realizing the true nature of their feelings toward each other.

As soon as this second part of the play has concluded, and before the critics can reassemble to dissect what they have just seen, a scene of chaos unfolds. Amelia Moreno and Baron Nuti are separately trying to go backstage in order to attack the actors who are portraying "them" because they do not recognize the interpretation of their lives being presented. They insist that they do not love each other and maintain this position to prove their innocence in the death of La Vela.

In the midst of this attempt to throw the theater into anarchy and in effect break the mirror that they believe has been reflecting a distorted picture of their lives, La Moreno and Baron Nuti encounter each other. Nuti is arguing that Pirandello has given his stage reflection words and actions that are contrary to his "reality" when La Moreno enters in heated argument with the play's Director:

THE DIRECTOR: But you know that neither the author nor the leading lady has ever met you.
LA MORENO: It was my own voice. And my gestures—all my own gestures. I saw myself—I saw myself up there.
THE DIRECTOR: That's because you wanted to see yourself.
LA MORENO: No! No! That's not true. It was horrible to see myself there, presented in that act. But how is it possible that I would embrace that man? *(Nuti suddenly becomes aware of her presence and lets out a scream as he raises his arm to hide his face.)* Oh, God! There he is, there he is!
BARON NUTI: Amelia, Amelia . . . *(There is general excitement among the spectators, who almost cannot believe their own eyes in seeing in front of them, live, the same characters and the same scene that they just viewed at the end of the second act. They express this astonishment both with facial grimaces and with brief whispered comments, and with a few exclamations.)*

88   *Dreams of Passion*

VOICES OF SPECTATORS: Oh, look! There they are, there—Oh! Oh!—Both of them—they are replaying the scene—Look, look—
LA MORENO *(raving to the people she is with)*: Let me go ahead! Let me go ahead!
HER FRIENDS: Yes, let's go, let's go!
BARON NUTI *(throwing himself at her)*: No, no! You must come with me! With me!
LA MORENO *(moving away from him)*: No! Leave me alone! Leave me alone! Assassin!
BARON NUTI: Don't repeat what they made you say up there!
LA MORENO: Leave me alone. I'm not afraid of you!
BARON NUTI: But its true, it's true that we must punish ourselves together! Didn't you hear? Now everyone knows it. Come away, come.
LA MORENO: No, leave me alone. Damn you! I hate you!
BARON NUTI: We are drowning in our own blood. Come, come! *(He carries her away....)*

This scene between Baron Nuti and Amelia Moreno is a shocking one. Pirandello's play has not only been closely based on their lives; it has also anticipated how they would act when they finally came together again. Art has mirrored life, not only as it has been lived and is being lived, but also how it will be lived in the future. Pirandello's play has taken the initiative and predicted, based on past activity and human nature, something that the individuals involved were unwilling to admit about their feelings toward each other.

This prediction also is a mirror image of the first choral interlude, since that interlude predicts how the real audience is probably reacting to Pirandello's play.

As the responses of La Moreno show, there is not a complete correspondence between the fictitious and the real scenes. While it is possible to infer from this lack of complete identity that the mirror in the form of the play is an imperfect one, I think Pirandello has something else in mind. Nuti has reacted to the crisis of the mirror image by realizing the true nature of his feelings toward La Moreno. She has resisted, however, and is still trying to maintain the image she generated to protect herself from the need to feel guilt for the suicide of the sculptor. Nuti will not allow her this escape and forces her to accompany him and acknowledge the love, rather than the hate, that binds them together.

In the characterizations of these two people can be found the primary responses to Pirandello's dramatic art. One of these responses is recognition and acceptance of the truth that has been shown on the stage. The other, as seen in La Moreno, is the refusal to accept insights that are valid. Despite their centrality to the drama, it is necessary to remember that Baron Nuti and Amelia Moreno are both members of the audience attending Pirandello's play. In fact, they can be seen to represent the leadership of the two factions of that audience: those who champion Pirandello's insights and those who deny their efficacy. Thus, Nuti and Moreno are mirror images of the real audience just as Rocca and La Morello are reflections of them.

An additional complication occurs in the designation of Amelia Moreno as an actress. As in *Six Characters* and later *Tonight We Improvise,* the people who should be most responsive to Pirandello's insights into the connection between theater and life, those who work in the theater, are often the most recalcitrant. Nothing can be taken for granted. All assumptions must be questioned, all surfaces probed. La Moreno refuses to recognize the interpretation created by Pirandello's words and Delia Morello's actions because it does not coincide with her self-image, a projection of self that has been created in a manner similar to a role she might enact for the stage. Even in the selection of small details, such as the profession of his characters, Pirandello enriches his play by extending and compounding his central metaphor.

After having developed a complex matrix of many mirror images, Pirandello ends *Each in His Own Way* with the same kind of startling originality that has characterized the rest of the play. After the confrontation between La Moreno and Baron Nuti results in their exit from the theater, the play cannot continue. The uproar generated by the attacks on the acting company by La Moreno and Nuti has caused the actors' departure as well. In the midst of general chaos the following exchanges mark the end of the play:

A STUPID SPECTATOR: And to think that they were considered rebels; and then they acted just like the characters in the play.

THE DIRECTOR: And she had the nerve to come to me and to attack the leading lady on the stage. "I, embrace that man?"
MANY: It's incredible! It's incredible!
AN INTELLIGENT SPECTATOR: But no, signori: it's completely natural. They saw themselves in a mirror and they rebelled, above all, at that final gesture.
THE DIRECTOR: But they repeated that very gesture!
THE INTELLIGENT SPECTATOR: Exactly. Right. They have, involuntarily, repeated before our eyes what art had predicted. *(The spectators voice their approval; someone applauds, others laugh.)*
THE COMIC ACTOR *(who comes forward from one of the doors that leads from the stage):* Don't believe that, signori. Those two there? Listen: I'm the comic actor who played, most convincingly, the part of Diego Cinci in the play. Those two have just left—But you have not seen the third act yet.
THE SPECTATORS: That's right—the third act. What happened in the third act!—tell us, tell us.
THE COMIC ACTOR: Eh, what things, what things. And after . . . after the third act . . . what things, what things. *(Having said this, he goes away.)*
THE MANAGER OF THE THEATER: Excuse me, sir, but as the Director, does it seem possible for the audience to remain here talking like this?
THE DIRECTOR: What do you want me to do? Make them clear out?
STAGE MANAGER: But the show cannot possibly continue. The actors have gone home.
THE DIRECTOR: Then why ask me? Make up a sign and send the people home.
THE MANAGER OF THE THEATER: But some of the audience is still seated in the auditorium.
THE DIRECTOR: All right. For the audience that is still there I'll go in front of the curtain and inform them with a couple of words.
THE MANAGER OF THE THEATER: Yes, yes, go, go, please *(while the Director proceeds toward the door to stage).* Please go away, go away, ladies and gentlemen. The play is over. *(The curtain is lowered, and as soon as it is the Director appears in front of it.)*
THE DIRECTOR: It grieves me to announce to the audience that due to the unpleasant incidents that took place at the end of the second act, the third act cannot be presented.

The possibility that the third act could not be performed has been suggested from the very beginning, with the note printed in the program. The note establishes that the author, because his play is based on the lives of real people, anticipates that their curiosity might attract them to the theater and result in some kind of disturbance. It is also quite possible this disturbance will be of a magnitude as to necessitate the premature conclusion of the evening.

Pirandello, as the actual author of the play within a play, has anticipated the possible emergency by making his two acts tell the complete story of his protagonists, Delia Morello and Michele Rocca. The appearance of the Comic Actor who plays Diego, omitted in the Livingston translation, is very important here, since his remarks suggest that the supposed third act would probably focus on him and thus be full of more misleading information. Although Diego does serve as a guide to some of Pirandello's pet ideas, he is ultimately superfluous, since the impact of those ideas comes not through his articulation of them but through their dramatization in the relationship between the onstage couple and their mirror image.

The identification of Diego's interpreter as the Comic Actor also supplies further evidence that he is not intended as a serious figure; his pronouncements were not to be taken as truth. An Italian acting company, as will be demonstrated in *Tonight We Improvise,* distributed roles according to character types. In the five plays being considered here, the Comic Actor would probably be cast as Laudisi, the Director in *Six Characters,* Diego, Doctor Hinkfuss in *Tonight We Improvise,* and Tito Belcredi in *Enrico IV.* All five embody positions comparable to the *avvertimento* level of response in *L'umorismo:* they apprehend only the surface reality of the situation under consideration. Their insights are incomplete and are ultimately rejected in favor of a more complex vision, one that combines the sympathy of emotional perception with the intellectuality of rational analysis.

The Comic Actor who has been portraying Diego is the perfect person to remind the audience of the third act. It is illusionary, a trap, the same as his contribution to the meaning of the play. As in *Six Characters,* Pirandello does not discard the three-act structure but rather uses it as part of his play's texture. Those members of the real audience who require a third act have obviously missed the point of *Each in His Own Way*. Pirandello makes that point, not only through his use of the *commedia a chiave* characters, but also through his techniques of *umorismo* as well. It is Amelia Moreno and Baron Nuti who force the transition from the surface level apprehended by the mere awareness of the *avvertimento* to the *sentimento* level, where thought and emotion combine to present a vision often contrary to the initial one. Once it is known that the play is both based on the lives of "real" people and is being viewed by those people, it cannot be dismissed as the kind of intellectual exercise that it first appears to be.

The choral interlude becomes vital because it demonstrates exactly how Pirandello's audience remains on the *avvertimento* level, dealing more with preconceived ideas of his dramatic practices than with any involvement in what they have just seen. The choral audience does not treat the characters of the first act of the play as people but as instruments for the playwright's ideology. One member of the audience antagonistic to what he has just seen even calls it "a game of enigmas." The *commedia a chiave* characters thus function to prove to the real audience how shallow these responses really are.

It is against this background of an audience relating only to the conceptual surface of his play, and not to the effect these ideas have on his characters, that Pirandello introduces his *commedia a chiave*. Baron Nuti and La Moreno must respond differently, since they apprehend the play on an emotional as well as an intellectual level. They have responded to the people Pirandello has created rather than to the ideas, to the suffering inherent in Delia Morello's situation rather than to the intellectual sparring of Diego Cinci and his two friends over the truth or falsity of their perceptions.

Since the characters of Delia Morello and Michele Rocca have been closely based on the lives of La Moreno and Baron Nuti, it may appear that their reaction to the stage images of themselves is a somewhat obvious device. To see the importance of the *commedia a chiave* only within the narrow limitations of its literal application, however, would be to underestimate Pirandello's insight. Is their intense personal involvement with the action onstage the only possible alternative to the superficial overintellectualizations of the stage audience? Of course not. By implication the play suggests a middle ground, a sensitive response that moves from *avvertimento* to *sentimento* with the realization that there may be contradictions between what one first judges a situation to be and how one reacts to that same event after further engagement. As Pirandello admits in his title, each person views the world in his or her own way. Yet despite the personal differences inherent in individual perception, the practice of *umorismo* will deepen the perception and make it less susceptible to error or superficiality.[7]

Pirandello labeled his theater a mirror theater because he wanted it to reflect human behavior. He also spoke of the crisis caused by the confrontation with the reflection seen in that mirror as the essence of his drama. Although the crisis of seeing a fiction modeled directly on their lives and predicting future activity is a shattering experience for La Moreno and Baron Nuti, it only points to the even more important crisis of the play: that of the real audience who must face its mirror image and confront the shallowness of its response to what has been presented before it.

In attempting to prove the necessity of the humoristic response to his audience so that it will not be satisfied with an intellectual curiosity limited to the surface apprehended by the *avvertimento* state of perception, Pirandello exposes the inadequacy of that curiosity on two levels. The suffering experienced by Delia Morello and Michele Rocca in the play and by Amelia Moreno and Baron Nuti in the "audience" prove the shallowness of the reaction of both the Palegari-Savio-Cinci group and the stage audience that discusses Pirandello's pessimism and intellectuality. The sympathetic perception of that suffering not only deepens the audience's response to the play but also contradicts the impressions that might have been conveyed initially.

Each in His Own Way is thus not what it first appears to be: either an elaborate enigma centering on the correct estimation of Delia Morello's motivation or a belabored reformulation of Pirandello's pet themes, presented here perhaps even more obviously than in the past. Instead of an intellectual exercise, Pirandello has created a drama of emotional involvement where on one level supposedly real people see themselves mirrored onstage, while on another level the actual audience should have a similar spark of recognition. By dramatizing the typical response to his work in the choral interludes, and by juxtaposing this response against a play that clearly demonstrates its inadequacies, Pirandello is attempting to dramatize *umorismo* so that his audience will understand what it is and why it is so necessary.

Pirandello's insistence on the use of his own name and public image is perhaps the ultimate way he tries to reach his audience. Since both the stage audience and the *commedia a chiave* characters are really fictional constructs, although on another level of reality in the play, Pirandello's injection of himself provides the closest correspondence to "reality." Moreover, it is with the use of his own persona as well as the theater that Pirandello establishes himself as a Modernist. He writes not just about the theater as an objective phenomenon but about his experience in it, using that experience as metaphor for what occurs in everyday life. He has dared to acknowledge the theater's existence as the setting of *Six Characters* and has been savagely attacked for his innovation. Now in *Each in His Own Way* he uses those attacks as the means of proving the necessity for the shifting perspectives he both advocates and dramatizes.

In mirroring the public response to his work, Pirandello shows why the theater is the necessary medium for his attempts at communication. The theater is by nature a public art, an art that fosters the sense of occasion in its audience. The individual member of the audience brings attitudes toward the playwright and the theater experience itself that have been formulated while part of a group. He is susceptible to the influence of the people around him in responding to the work he is presently watching. The first choral interlude makes clear that the speakers are not merely responding to what they have just seen but are reacting to Pirandello as a cultural figure and are doing so for the benefit of those people who are listening to them. People find it impossible to react to a given phenomenon solely on the basis of what they experience at the moment, but base their judgments on a myriad of past experiences and present circumstances. It is Pirandello's point that the response to his work has been, for whatever reason, the opposite of what it should have been. He is not searching for approbation but for a response that recognizes the reality of his work, a response that penetrates through the surface to concentrate on the effects ideas have on the emotional life of his characters and not on the ideas themselves as theoretical abstractions.

The disruption of the play within a play at the end of *Each in His Own Way* is the culmination of Pirandello's artistic statement, since it illustrates the difficulty of embodying truth in art, of showing an audience an image of itself that it will recognize as true. If the artist makes his characters and situations too generalized, then it will be easy for the audience to effect the kind of evasions that shield them from making any connection with the image reflected from the stage. If that image is too specific, however, the very accuracy of the mirror will necessitate its smashing, just as the pain of seeing their inner nature violated caused Amelia Moreno and Baron Nuti to attack the actors who had been impersonating them and disrupt the performance.

By using his own name and dramatic style as the example, Pirandello personalizes the dilemma and makes it more accessible. In choosing the artistic medium closest to life itself, he may have the means to show his audience the most direct image of themselves, but he also risks the most immediate danger of group evasion or disruption. The artist—and by implication anyone else who challenges others to reject their superficial impressions in favor of the deeper reality underneath, with the probable contradiction of that previous perception, that is, the humorist—should not expect to be welcome.

5.

Tonight We Improvise (1929)

After having focused on the characters who form the play and the audience that witnesses it, Pirandello turns to the crucial medium of the actors for the final part of his theater trilogy. *Tonight We Improvise (Questa sera si recita a soggetto)* explores the actor's relationship to the director and to his fellow actors. The key examination, however, centers on the actor's relationship to the material he must interpret and bring to life—the character whom he creates on the stage. While this problem was vividly dramatized in the Madam Pace scene and its dramatic re-creation in *Six Characters*, it becomes the central concern here, seen from the actor's viewpoint rather than the character's.

In order to explore the actor's relationship with his character in a way that allows as much latitude as possible, Pirandello chooses the theatrical technique of improvisation as the subject matter of his play. As with *Each in His Own Way*, however, *Tonight We Improvise* represents the premiere of a new work, performed in front of an audience, and not under rehearsal conditions. The actors' lack of familiarity with the process, and their need to be perfectly in tune with the characters to create their words, gestures, and emotions, cause difficulties that a normal script does not offer. These difficulties often force the actors to abandon their characterizations and appear as themselves.

The sense of the creation of a performance is emphasized, embodying in the theatrical level of the play a theme that will then be extended outward. The actors' need to take control of the improvisatory process, reinforced by the dangers of improvisation as illustrated by the play's conclusion, allows Pirandello to continue his dramatization of the connection between theater and life. In fact, the premise that there is no established script makes *Tonight We Improvise* a more accurate mirror of offstage life than a set text, where all words and actions are established in advance. The confusion created by the actors' attempts to improvise their play mirrors the chaos and ambiguity of life itself. Dr. Hinkfuss, the director and orginator of the project, tries to exert control over the actors as well as the entire enterprise, but he fails because the actors cannot be manipulated in the way he envisions. Once the actors have been given the responsibility of creating their characters and, more important, the words of those characters, they make demands and become entangled in ways that would not arise in the performance of a regular script.

Tonight We Improvise is thus both a continuation and extension of the theater trilogy. Theater is still reflecting life but is now doing it more accurately, since improvisation is one step closer to "reality." The director's loss of control reflects the belief that life becomes fragmented and disrupted by the constant struggle between the freedom of impulse and the constraint of form. But more important, it extends the interpenetration of life and theater that lies at the core of Pirandello's dramaturgy. Furthermore, the self-conscious use of improvisation as the theatrical technique mirroring the form-flux dichotomy in life is yet another indication that his theater is a Modernist one. Life and theater not only reflect each other but do so in a contest insisting on the theatrical identity of both.

As with the previous two trilogy plays, Pirandello also inserts himself into this one. Dr. Hinkfuss has adapted one of his short stories, dealing with life in a small Sicilian city, into the scenario the actors must improvise on. Once this mention of the playwright is made, however, it is not referred to again. Having emphasized himself as a central figure in *Each in His Own Way,* Pirandello shifts the focus to Hinkfuss as the creative artist attempting to exercise control.

Hinkfuss explains his project to both the actors and the audience and then continually interrupts the actors' attempts to follow his instructions. He won't relinquish control even though he wants the spontaneity and verisimilitude of improvisation. After he is finally ejected by the actors, who then proceed to improvise the final scenes of his "play," he returns to inform them not only that has he watched their work but that he has been responsible for the lighting effects that contributed to its success. The almost fatal consequences of the close identification between the Leading Actress and Mommina, the character she has created, prove, however, the dangers involved in this kind of theatrical endeavor.

The scenario Hinkfuss creates for his actors deals with a family dominated by the mother, Donna Ignazia, also known as the "General." Whereas her husband tries to escape his wife's domineering by taking refuge in a local "jazz cabaret," Donna Ignazia and her four daughters entertain officers from the local air force base and try to amuse themselves despite an atmosphere they find hostile to the kind of activities they enjoy. Mommina, the oldest daughter and a promising singer, is in love with Rico Verri, one of the airmen, who is extremely jealous of her talent, her friends, and her family. After the father dies she marries Verri, who forces her to become isolated from all contact with her family, her music, and everything else that he cannot totally dominate. In the last scene Mommina tells her children of her past hopes for a career in opera. She is then visited by her family, including a younger sister who has become an opera star, and finally dies from the strain these confrontations and Verri's treatment have placed on her.

A strong sense of confusion is created by the constant movement back and forth between the two realities of the actors improvising a play for Dr. Hinkfuss and the audience and the world of the play itself. This confusion suggests themes that Pirandello has explored in much of his previous work, specifically the lack of coherence in the human personality and in the individual's perception of himself and of outside phenomena. The chaos here, however, is particularly Italian. Not since his early Sicilian dialect plays, in fact, has Pirandello written a play that uses the Italian national characteristics so specifically. The use of improvisation itself is evident in one of the major Italian contributions to world theater, the commedia dell'arte. Although the characters here may not be the masks of the Renaissance comedy, they do embody stereotypes of Italian life: the insanely jealous lover, the overbearing wife, the woman who is treated like a slave by her husband.

It is not in the melodramatic aspects of this play, however, that Pirandello infuses the main thrust of its Italianness; the basic situations of the previous trilogy plays also contain relationships of passion and personal honor that are more easily understood, given the Mediterranean temperament. The short story on which the improvisation is based deals with family life in a Sicilian town, so that many of the central details of the "improvised play" are drawn from Italian mores. The uses of religion, in a procession that signals the start of the "play" and in Donna Ignazia's recitation of the Ave Maria in order to cure herself of a toothache, and the importance of opera to the La Croce family are but two instances of significant elements of Italian culture contributing to the basic fabric of the play.

Pirandello wrote and premiered this play in Berlin, having left Italy because he felt unappreciated there. The distance from his native milieu, along with the desire to communicate the specifics of the milieu to members of a foreign culture, might have contributed to his choice of material. There are more important textual considerations, however, for this choice. Of the three trilogy plays, this one attempts the most complete exploration of the line between order and chaos. If, in the past, art has represented a more ordered existence, with life the embodiment of uncontrolled activity, this play, with its choice of the freer form of improvisation, moves toward the blurring of the distinctions. By having the actors create their roles as they go along, Pirandello makes theater seem closer to life. As a counterbalance, he uses the practices of religion and opera to show the theatricality of Italian life. Pirandello may not be ready for the categorical statement that life is theater and theater is life, but this play moves further in that direction than the two previous theater trilogy works or, for that matter, any other play in his canon, although he achieves a similar synthesis in *Enrico IV* through a different approach.

The ambiguity between the theatricality of life and the reality of theater in this play is grounded in its improvisatory frame. The ability of the actors to break character and appear as themselves (the stage directions dictate that the actors are to use their real names in referring to each other) allows the possibility of a constant shift of reference point. In the first part of the play the shifts are frequent; in the latter part, the improvised play is allowed to proceed for lengthy stretches, so that an interruption by Dr. Hinkfuss or by the actors themselves jolts the audience back into the realization that they are watching actors creating a play. When the Leading Actress faints after she has played her big scene, this ambiguity is brought to a climax, so that neither actors nor audience are sure if it is the actress herself or the actress in character, or perhaps even the actress playing the "actress," who is ill and, for a moment, possibly dead.

As I have suggested in the previous chapters, in his plays Pirandello uses the theory of *umorismo* both literally and metaphorically. He is interested in exploring the possiblity that what appears comic at first may indeed have its serious side. This juxtaposition or combination of the laughable and the pathetic, if not of the tragic, places Pirandello firmly in the tradition of tragicomedy that dominates late-nineteenth-century and twentieth-century drama. As the possibility of making clear distinctions disappears in such fields as politics, religion, philosophy, psychology, and physics, drama—the mirror image of the world that contains these disciplines—must keep pace. The clearly definable genres of comedy and tragedy lose their relevance to the contemporary playwright; the masks of the two types of drama merge into one ambiguous expression, poised between the smile and the frown.[1]

Umorismo also establishes the need to penetrate beyond surfaces in order to perceive the reality underneath. This reality, often the opposite of what a first impression may suggest, is discovered by moving from a purely intellectual apprehension of the phenomenon to a more sympathetic vision encompassing emotion as well as intellect. Although some of the plays, like *That's the Way Things Are*, present a fairly clear dichotomy, others create a more elusive relationship between the various levels. By an improvisatory technique that allows a frequent change between actor and character reality, and through the specific practices of Italian culture that make the distinction between life and theater even less firm, *Tonight We*

Improvise becomes one of Pirandello's most complex and indeed most humoristic plays.

Although there were reflections and reverberations back and forth among the three levels of the fictional characters, the stage audience and the *commedia a chiave* figures in *Each in His Own Way*, that play employed a basically linear pattern, working its way from the surface of the "play" to the deeper reality of the two people who were watching themselves re-created on the stage. In *Tonight We Improvise* the changes from one level of reality to another are less organized. The presence of Hinkfuss and the actors' uncertainty about the new technique they are using insures the constant possibility that the current reality will be interrupted and another, no less real, situation will be substituted. The actors, using their real names and their position in the company, such as the Leading Lady and Leading Man, the Character Actress or the old Comic Actor, create one kind of reality, while the *soggeto*, the scenario of Sicilian life, establishes another. Pirandello has firmly anchored his fiction in Italian reality so that the improvised scenes must be played realistically, providing an alternative but no less absorbing reality to the struggles of the actors among themselves and with their director.

With *Tonight We Improvise*, therefore, Pirandello emphasizes the need for constant attention to what lies underneath the surface by constantly shifting the perspective on that surface. He begins with an overintellectual director who likes to deliver long, philosophical lectures to the audience. He then adds a melodramatic scenario and an acting company uncertain about the theatrical technique they have been asked to employ. From this base, however, he develops an exploration of the theater-life relationship and of aspects of Italian life that suggests a deeper seriousness beyond what may appear on the surface. What first gives the impression of being frivolously irrelevant is reexamined until a new attitude is suggested. The theater has become more prism than mirror, except that instead of merely showing another angle or perspective, Pirandello follows the route of *umorismo* to suggest that what may appear to be unimportant can have a real effect on human beings, whose emotions as well as intellect are involved.

From the initial moment of the play, when the sound of actors arguing behind the curtain is heard by the audience in the auditorium, one senses an atmosphere of ambiguity. A planted audience member suggests that there is a fight in progress, while another answers, "Perhaps it's part of the play." The lack of certainty characteristic of Pirandello's previous work is now completely encapsulated by his dramatic form. The use of the voices from the audience is another suggestion of the breakdown of clear distinctions, forcing the real audience to ponder the identity of the people speaking. The arrival of the director, Dr. Hinkfuss, complicates matters, with his explanation of the premise of the evening's activities and his statement to an actor in the audience that his remarks are part of the play.

Dr. Hinkfuss embodies in himself the sense of ambiguity and *contrario* to be established throughout the play. He is described as having:

> ... the most terrible and unjust misfortune of being a tiny man, little taller than the length of an arm. He tries to avenge himself by wearing his hair extremely long. The first thing that one notices about him is his hands, which arouse disgust perhaps even in him, because they are so thin, with fingers that are very pale and covered with hair, like caterpillars.

This grotesque man, dressed in formal evening clothes, proceeds to lecture the audience on the nature of theater and its relationship to life. While some may argue that art avenges itself on life by creating a certainty that is impossible in life, Dr. Hinkfuss believes art is brought to life because each person approaching an individual work of art views it differently. Although a critic like Robert Brustein may identify Hinkfuss as one of Pirandello's *raisonneur* spokesmen,[2] the playwright has undercut his character dramatically, first by making him a freak of nature, and later by having him thrown out of his own production by his actors, who can no longer tolerate his interference.[3]

Pirandello is thought to have based his characterization of Hinkfuss on Max Reinhardt, the famous German director, who had directed the German production of *Six Characters*. Pirandello objected to the concept of the star director who imposed his interpretation on a text in a way similar to the characters' objections to the actors' interpretations of them in *Six Characters*. When he was allowed to fulfill his dream and given his own theater in Rome, Pirandello is said to have directed his own plays and those of other authors in a very straightforward manner, emphasizing the text as written by the playwright. This theater, Il Teatro D'arte di Roma, was founded in 1925 with money provided by Mussolini, but had a short life span due to financial difficulties.

As soon as the actors themselves appear on stage, another aspect of the basic problem inherent in improvisation manifests itself. Even before the improvised play begins, the old Character Actress who takes the role of the mother, Donna Ignazia, has been slapping the old Comic Actor, who plays her husband. She argues that the slapping is a natural part of her character, while he asks whether it is not "real" rather than "acted." The question of how much freedom improvisation allows the actor leads to the more serious one of how the distinction can be made in such activity between what is done as part of character and what is done for personal reasons. As this argument between the two old actors indicates, the possibility that the lines between theater and life will become blurred under the circumstances of Dr. Hinkfuss's experiment is a real one. Improvisation can create a reality that is closer to the confusion of life outside the theater, but that confusion can also threaten the basic discipline of the project and lead to chaos.[4]

With the introduction of the other characters and the basic situation of the improvised play, yet another problem unfolds. The actors tend to use the information they have been given about their characters too quickly. Hinkfuss tells them not to anticipate what should develop in the course of the play. The short story he has chosen as the basis of the scenario allows him to impose certain limits on his actors' improvisation. Within that framework, however, he has less control than he would like over the unfolding of his drama. A tension has been created. Hinkfuss wants to use improvisation, and yet he also wants the results of the actors' work to coincide with his vision. He is trying for a synthesis of freedom and control that the play ultimately shows to be impossible, especially when the two constituent parties have different visions both of what the final result should be and of how it should be achieved.

It is only after the theatrical aspect of *Tonight We Improvise* has been firmly established, with the introduction of the characters (and their enacters), that Pirandello begins to present the fiction in which these characters will participate. Dr. Hinkfuss does not proceed directly with the story itself, however. His improvised play begins with a religious procession, including altar boys, young girls, the Holy Family, and other religious figures. Domenico Vittorini argues that this procession proves that Dr. Hinkfuss does not trust the story he is presenting and feels the need to create Sicilian local color by the creation of a tableau.[5] While I agree that this procession helps to establish the importance of religion in Sicilian life, there is a more important reason for its inclusion. The procession is a performance, with townspeople playing characters, for example, an old man and a young woman dressed as Mary and Joseph. By showing the affinity that real-life religious practices have to theater, Pirandello is presenting a counterpoint to the reality of the theater that he has previously demonstrated in his insistence upon introducing the actors as themselves as well as in their roles as characters.

The procession also demonstrates that role playing occurs on many levels and occasions. The old man and young woman participationg in the pageant are not really actors by profession; yet they are fulfilling that function here, even if they do not see themselves in such a way. The procession may be primarily an act of faith, but it is also spectacle, a presentation to be viewed by an audience. Life has become theatricalized, just as Hinkfuss's theater has appropriated its interlude from Sicilian life.

As soon as the procession, with its chant praising God and the Virgin Mary, is completed, the scene suddenly shifts to a jazz cabaret. The swift jolt from the timelessness of the religious ceremony to the contemporaneity of the jazz cabaret, with the total change in mood from sacred to profane such a change entails, is an example of Pirandello's use of the *contrario* on a superficial level. Yet humanity's need for spectacle, for an escape into the costume and milieu offered by such rituals, is an important point in this play. All three of the trilogy plays examine the role of the theater as a mirror of life; but in *Tonight We Improvise* the vision of life as theater is explored with a complexity and directness lacking in the other two works. The need to participate in other realities, whether they are in the form of religious ceremony, theatrical presentation, or the adoption of an individual mask, is of course a central concern in the Pirandellian canon. As the plays suggest, it is the use of such performance techniques that makes the definition of reality or truth so difficult.

The scene in the jazz cabaret illustrates how the characters of the improvised play use their other realities for escape. The old man, Sampognetta, who later becomes almost a dramatic incarnation of the grotesquely made up old woman in *L'umorismo,* patronizes the cabaret to escape the abuse to which his wife subjects him at home. He is a strange creature who whistles whenever he is made uncomfortable by people who make fun of him. Even though all the customers of the cabaret mock him, the singer he comes to see does not. He is inebriated and rather ridiculous, but she still has both affection and pity for him. He alone takes her singing, and the emotions she expresses in her art, seriously. For him, the created reality of art is authentic. One of the customers tells him that the singer's tears are not real. To the statement, "She does that for a living, Signor Palmiro! Do not believe in those tears," Sampognetta replies:

(denying seriously, also with his finger): No, no, ah, no, no! What profession! What profession! I give you my word of honor that the woman suffers: she suffers for real. And now she has the same kind of voice as my oldest daughter, what a voice! And she has confided in me that she is also from a very good family.

The old man wants to believe in the reality of the singer's suffering, since it is real for him, especially as it reminds him of his daughter, who also sings both to mask and to express pain. The cabaret singer may see the old man as a father figure, but at the very least she finds in him someone who elevates her art by taking it seriously, and who may comprehend its truth in a way the more sophisticated patrons do not. Earlier in the scene she has been moved to pity the old man when the others played a trick on him by attaching paper horns to his head.[6] The old man himself had joined in their laughter until he discovered that he was the butt of their joke. Sampognetta, here and in his death scene later, is the character who is perhaps closest to the pure embodiment of *umorismo.* In a play where the reality of appearances and the falsity of artifices are challenged and interchanged, this use of such a humorous character adds another dimension to the vision Pirandello creates.

The use of juxtaposition in this play is one of its sharpest elements. It occurs in the shifts between actors and the characters they enact, and also between groupings of characters within the improvised play, when individual scenes comment on each other by their proximity. As Sampognetta is thrown out of the nightclub by the other patrons, he encounters his wife and four daughters, who are on the way to their temple of escape, the opera. In her customary manner, Ignazia bitterly castigates her husband, while the daughters are more sympathetic. After a near fight between the family and their escorts and the customers of the bar, Ignazia and her entourage proceed to the opera. As the scenery is changed for the opera house, Dr. Hinkfuss appears for the first time since the beginning of the act. He merely assists in the transition from one scene to another, but his presence serves as a reminder that Sampognetta, Ignazia, and all the rest are characters in a play being improvised by actors.

The arrival of Ignazia and her family at the opera house disrupts the audience there, which is already seated and watching the performance. Even in the theater itself there is chaos, with an altercation between the La Croces and the opera audience mirroring the one in the street moments earlier. The scenes in the cabaret and opera house indicate the impossibility of escape from the imbroglios of everyday life, even in those places designed for such escape. Pirandello is making his point about the theater as a place of confrontation in a much different way than he did in *Each in His Own Way,* employing more comedy and exaggeration here. He still affirms nonetheless that life and theater feed off and reflect each other and therefore cannot be separated, since both borrow from each other in creating their reality.

Behind the subject matter and the technique that Pirandello has been using to express these ideas, both in this play and the others under discussion here, is the underlying assumption of the fragmentation of modern life, of modern society. Pirandello devises a dramatic effect in the middle of *Tonight We Improvise* that brilliantly illustrates this fragmentation. During the intermission of the opera performance at which the La Croce family is in attendance, an intermission for *Tonight We Improvise* occurs as well. During this intermission, the La Croce women and their male companions mingle with the real audience in various parts of the theater's lobby, while Dr. Hinkfuss prepares a scenic display on the stage. The actors, in character, simultaneously participate in five conversations that reveal nothing new about the plot, or even about character relationships, but that reinforce what has been revealed previously. Hinkfuss even elicits from planted audience members a summary of what occurred in the lobby for the benefit of those who have remained in the auditorium.[7]

This intermezzo establishes in both words and dramatic action the momentary and ephemeral nature of the theatrical experience and, by extension, of life itself. Here, literally as well as figuratively, certain members of the audience have not seen and heard the same things that others have. Although the theatrical experience usually orders life so that the audience sees everything, or at least all members see the same things, Pirandello conducts a daring experiment in the middle of this play in order to suggest the limited nature of our experiences. At the same time, he is also blurring the distinctions between life and art by having the two intermissions coincide, with members of both levels of reality sharing the same lobby.

After the interlude of the intermission scenes, the third act begins with a religious ceremony and an operatic performance. As the curtain rises, Ignazia is reciting the Ave Maria in an attempt to cure a toothache. The Ave Maria tableau, complete with quavering candle and green mood light, is interrupted by the wild arrival of Totina, who enters dressed in one of the airmen's uniforms, singing in an attempt to divert her mother from her pain. She only disrupts the ritual that is in progress. When Mommina later also sings to distract her mother's attention from the pain, her performance is interrupted by the return of Rico Verri, who has been sent to the pharmacy for medicine. Verri becomes enraged at Mommina's singing, since she had promised him that she would discontinue it, and he becomes embroiled in a fight with the La Croce women and some of the airmen visiting them. During that fight Ignazia assumes the role of martyr and Mommina that of victim, as both women try to find ways to justify their behavior.

The theatrical quality of Italian life is evident here. Ignazia gives a long tirade in which she says she is dying and asks God to allow her suffering to atone for her daughters' amusement. She encourages their singing so that she can at least enjoy vicariously, before she dies, the pleasure she claims has been denied to her. Each new moment in the scene interrupts one kind of performance with another of a different kind. The characters shift from farce to melodrama, both of which have their roots in Pirandello's sense of the excesses of Italian behavior. Some moments are consciously theatrical, such as Totina's and Mommina's singing and even the religious ritual of the Ave Maria. Others, like Rico's rantings and the martyr speech of Ignazia, are self-dramatizing, although not intended to be viewed as performances. Yet even if such actions are not consciously melodramatic, they appear that way to outside observers, that is, an audience.

The chaos of the scene between the La Croce women and the airmen transgresses the boundaries of the improvised theatrical form. As Mommina, the Leading Actress improvises a line she should have saved until later and thereby precipitates a general attack on Verri. He explodes, as actor rather than as character, and the tensions that had been building within the scene now are transferred to the relationships between the actors. The actors are living their characters and want the freedom to say whatever seems appropriate at a particular moment. This freedom leads to chaos, however, since it is theatrically impossible for all the actors to guide the scene in the directions that their feelings lead them.

As Dr. Hinkfuss attempts to mediate this argument, the reality of the play reasserts itself. The old character actor enters, besmirched with blood so that he can play his death scene as Sampognetta. He has been knocking at the door, the cue for his entrance, but has been ignored because the actors have been arguing among themselves over the proper way to continue their improvisation. The old man is a comic actor. A death scene is an extremely difficult task for him. Now his fellow actors are making it even more difficult by their refusal to continue the scene that prepares for his appearance onstage.

The death scene of Sampognetta is perhaps the best illustration of Pirandello's skill in merging the realities of actor and character in this play. After the old actor complains about waiting for his knocking to be acknowledged, order is restored and he is allowed to reenter, in character, and begin his scene, one that is both comic and pathetic at the same time. Sampognetta has been wounded defending the honor of the cabaret singer, who now accompanies him home along with one of the patrons of the cabaret. The paradox Pirandello has set up—that of the death scene of a comic actor—brings to a climax the *umorismo* first suggested in the jazz cabaret. As the old actor creates Sampognetta's death scene, the reality of the actor is juxtaposed against the reality of the character, resulting in a synthesis that contains aspects of both but that ultimately is even more moving because of the comic surface being contradicted.[8]

After Sampognetta makes his second entrance, he is initially silent while the family sends for a doctor and tries to attend to him. He is also smiling, something that disturbs his family, since "it isn't natural," even when he has been drinking. They beg him to explain this smile, and when he does he shifts from the level of character to that of actor:

SAMPOGNETTA: Because it pleases me to see how much better than I you all are.
VERRI *(while the others look each other in the eye, all of a sudden stopped in their game):* But what are you talking about?
SAMPOGNETTA: I say that I, like this, without knowing how I got into the house, if no one came to let me in, after having knocked at the door—
DR. HINKFUSS *(getting up from his seat, angrily):* Still on this? Again?
SAMPOGNETTA: I cannot die, Signor Director; I start to laugh, seeing how good they all are, and I cannot die. The maid *(looking around for her)*—where is she? I do not see her—she was supposed to run and announce: "Oh, God. The master! Oh, God, the master! They're carrying him home wounded!"
DR. HINKFUSS: But what does this matter now? Hasn't your entrance into the house already been established?
SAMPOGNETTA: All right, then we will establish my death in the same way and won't talk about it any further.
DR. HINKFUSS: That is impossible. You must speak and act out the scene, and die!
SAMPOGNETTA: Very well, here goes the scene. *(He stretches out on the couch.)* I'm dead.

DR. HINKFUSS: But not that way.

SAMPOGNETTA *(leaping to his feet and coming forward)*: Dear Signor Director, you come up here and finish killing me off. What more can I say—I repeat that, by myself, I cannot die the way you want me to die. I am not an accordion, which expands and contracts, and when you press the keys, out comes a tune.

DR. HINKFUSS: But your colleagues—

SAMPOGNETTA *(quickly)*: They are better than I am. I said that and it pleases me to say it. I cannot do it. For me the entrance is everything. You wanted to skip it. . . . I needed that cry by the maid to set myself up. And Death must enter with me, presenting itself amid the shameless revelry of my house: Death the drunk, as has been established; drunk from a wine that has made blood. And I had to speak, yes, I know, to communicate somehow amid the horror of all this—I—taking courage from the wine and the blood, hanging on to this woman *(He attaches himself to the singer and leans on her, his arm around her neck)* like this—and I had to say foolish, incoherent things to my wife here, and my daughters and these young men, in order to prove to them that if I acted the part of the fool, it was because they were bad: a bad wife, bad daughters, bad friends. No, I'm not foolish; no, I am the only one who is good, and they are all bad. I am the only one who is smart and they are all stupid. Me, in my ingenuity, and them in their perverse bestiality; yes, yes *(becoming more enraged, as if someone were contradicting what he is saying)*, I am intelligent, intelligent the way babies are—not all of them, just those who grow up sad, amid the bestiality of their parents. But I had to say these things as a drunk, in a delirium; and then rub my bloody hands on my face, like this—and cover myself with blood. *(He turns to the company.)* Am I besmirched? *(after they nod affirmatively)*. Good. *(He now starts up again.)* And I then terrified you and made you cry—with real tears—and with a whistle that I can no longer do, puckering my lips like this. *(He tries to whistle but it does not come: fhh, fhh.)* To make my last whistle, and then, here. *(He calls one of the audience members of the cabaret to come over to him.)* Come here, you too. *(He puts his other arm around his shoulder.)* Thus, amid you two—but closer to you, my lovely one, I bend my chin—like the birds do—and I die. *(He rests his chin on the singer's breast; a few seconds later his arm slackens and he falls to the ground, dead.)*

Sampognetta's death scene evokes many aspects of the actor's art and the way in which that art creates its effects. From the beginning of the scene the old man insists that Hinkfuss is making it impossible for him to perform something that would be difficult for him under the best of circumstances. Hinkfuss assumes the position that we have seen others take in earlier plays, that of the unperceptive person who is interested only in an act itself and not in the ramifications of that act. For Hinkfuss the surface, in this case the death scene that will propel the action of the play forward, is all that matters; the artistic needs of the actor are of no concern.

One of the criticisms that has been leveled at Pirandello is that he does not create real characters, but rather puppets, whom he manipulates in order to communicate his ideas. While he does not try to answer that charge here, as he does with other charges in other plays, it becomes an issue in the relationship between Hinkfuss and the actors. Hinkfuss is not really interested in the actors as human beings or artists. He is both unaware of, and unconcerned with, their problems, exacerbated in this case by their use of a new acting technique. Both Sampognetta's anger and his wit are thus directed at Hinkfuss, who frustrates him by asking for a performance that the old man thinks he is unable to give. Just as certain of Pirandello's characters try to force roles or masks on others in order to make them conform to society's vision, so Hinkfuss wants a particular effect from the old man and is totally unaware of the time and preparation the actor needs in order to create it.

Sampognetta proves his superiority to Hinkfuss in two ways. When he agrees to play the death scene and merely says "I'm dead" and collapses on the couch, he outmaneuvers the director in a game of one-upsmanship. Hinkfuss has no way of forcing the old actor to give him what he wants. When Sampognetta finally decides on his own to attempt the death scene, he proves his superiority to Hinkfuss by showing what is involved in the art of acting. Proceeding step by step through the death scene, he uses the imperfect tense and the infinitive to emphasize that he, as actor, is demonstrating what he would have to do in order to play the scene as requested by the director. As Sampognetta does this, the strange magic of the theater takes over. Although he is still distancing himself from the character by the words he uses, at the same time he fuses his identity with that character. By the end of the scene, from both the reactions of the other actor/characters and the concentration of Sampognetta himself, there is no doubt that he is playing the scene, even if he still talks about how he should or would play it.

In the actor, who is at least two people whenever he is on stage, Pirandello has found the perfect metaphor for the fragmentation and multiplicity of the personality. In this scene, moreover, he has captured a moment that dramatizes this "schizophrenia," a moment in which the actor becomes someone else and yet remains himself. As Sampognetta details the steps that lead to his death, he is both actor and character. The line that separates the two has in one sense been erased, since at the moment of death he has become the old man, turning against his family and friends and leaning on the singer, the one person who has taken him seriously. Yet the language is so structured as to prevent a complete merging of actor and character. The audience is thus kept aware of the fact that it is watching a performance.

Through the character of Sampognetta, Pirandello achieves the essence of *umorismo*, both in terms of the character and also in terms of theatrical reality. Sampognetta is played by a comic actor, whose mock attempt at a death scene is the jocular "I'm dead." When he attempts a serious death scene, however, he shows the real tragedy of the character and the reality of his suffering at the hands of his family. The *sentimento del contrario* is achieved not only in the character of Sampognetta but also on a broader theatrical level. As audience we know that the character is not real, since the actor insists on this point; yet despite this fact the actor does create the reality of that character, so that both the other actors and the audience are involved and even moved by the death of this strange, even grotesque figure. It almost appears that Pirandello uses a distancing technique here for the exact opposite purpose of the alienation process employed by Bertolt Brecht. If Brecht wanted audience distancing to discourage emotional involvement and identification with the character, Pirandello seems to be attempting to demonstrate that the nature of the theater is such that emotion can be created and communicated despite our realization that actor and character are separate.

The complexity with which Pirandello constructs Sampognetta's death scene offers insight into both his thematic concerns and his dramatic technique. The conflict between the director and the actor continues the dramatization of *umorismo,* opposing the pragmatic intellectual with the character who suffers. Yet the conflict exists on two levels, since Sampognetta opposes Hinkfuss both as an actor and as a character. The old Comic Actor is not Sampognetta and thus must be assisted as he attempts to play his death scene. At the same time, he is an accomplished enough actor to create an illusion and make it real, merging his personality with that of his characterization. For Pirandello the mask and the face it covers often become indistinguishable. Here he offers a brilliant theatrical incarnation of this insight, transforming actor into character through a gradual process of transference. It is virtually impossible to mark the final transition between actor and character, just as it is often impossible to differentiate between mask and face or theater and life.

Pirandello's bold approach to dramaturgy is exemplified by his juxtaposition of the reemergence of Dr. Hinkfuss with the stunning moment of the death of Sampognetta. Just as the La Croce women begin to lament the old man's death, Hinkfuss leaps up from his seat, shouting, "Very good! Strike that scene! Strike that scene!— Blackout! *(The stage goes dark.)* Everyone offstage—The four sisters and the mother, around the dining room table—six days later—kill the living-room, give me light for the dining-room lamp." Hinkfuss's interruption proves his lack of sensitivity to the reality being created by his actors. He even informs the audience that while the effect has not been completely achieved tonight, it will be tomorrow. Hinkfuss is a tradesman constructing a product, while his actors are trying to bring their characters to life in a way that will be believable, both for themselves and for the audience.

While the women are offstage changing into mourning costumes, Hinkfuss informs the audience of the differences in interpretation of the character of Mommina between himself and the Leading Actress. While this is a common strain of the three theater plays, it is given particular prominence here. These differences contribute to the actors' revolt that occurs when they return. They do not want to continue the performance, and they give Hinkfuss an ultimatum: either he leaves the theater or they will cease the performance. They refuse to play marionettes for him any longer.

Hinkfuss has tempted his actors with the illusion of a freedom they have never before had: the freedom to create the words of their characters, and thus the characters themselves, and the resultant play in the course of performing it. Instead of really allowing them to do this, he has tried to control and shape the play. The actors have seen in improvisation the possibility of creating a piece of art very close to life itself, one that breathes and changes according to the vagaries of the moment. Even with a set character and an outline, the play would be as unpredictable and in a way as real as life. Perhaps because he realizes the impossibility of a work of art mirroring life so closely, Hinkfuss has tried to allow his actors as much freedom as possible while still constructing an artifice that will serve as an organizing principle for the material.

Pirandello is posing a dilemma, a *contrario,* with no real solution. The actors want a purity that is probably impossible, while Hinkfuss is attempting a synthesis that may be equally unworkable. Yet the problem is more than an artistic or theatrical one. Throughout Pirandello's works we have seen characters trying to organize life, to assert their viewpoint or to stop an interpretation they find either dangerous or displeasing. Much of life's conflict, as viewed through Pirandello's plays, is the struggle between different perspectives. Sometimes the playwright suggests that one vision has more validity than another (especially when the less valid viewpoint theatens to increase the suffering of others), while at other times he merely presents the clash between the two. Here the expulsion of Hinkfuss indicates the importance of self-expression to the actors. The director has not really tried to understand the ideas and emotions of either the actors or their characters, and now they must act in order to protect their viewpoint.

The arguments used by the actors in their confrontation with Hinkfuss stress the emotional aspects of their characters. They speak of the "passion" they have created for their characters in terms of childbirth, with the subsequent claim that no one, not even the director-playwright organizing the event, can command that life. When Hinkfuss challenges their right to evict him from his own theater, they answer him in the following way:

THE CHARACTER ACTRESS (Ignazia): When one lives a passion, that is the real theater, and then the merest outline is sufficient.
THE LEADING ACTRESS (Mommina): You cannot joke with passions.

THE LEADING ACTOR (Verri): You can manipulate every detail in order to obtain an effect only with insignificant farces.
EVERYONE ELSE: Go away! Go away!
DR. HINKFUSS: I am your director!
THE LEADING ACTOR: No one has control over life that has been given birth.
THE CHARACTER ACTRESS: Even the writer has to obey it.
THE COMIC ACTOR (Sampognetta): And good riddance to anyone who wants to give orders.
EVERYONE ELSE: Go away! Go away!
DR. HINKFUSS *(with his back to the door):* I'll make a formal protest. This is scandalous. I am your direc . . .

Hinkfuss is interfering with the actors' relationship with their characters, and when he refuses to understand the feelings involved in that relationship, they force him from the theater.

While the actors are being used to dramatize the themes of interpretation, multiplicity, and fragmentation, they also embody the need to balance emotion and intellect. Hinkfuss has tried to organize the play according to what he considers to be a logical, rational approach. (His opening monologue has established his credentials as an intellectual.) Yet the characters being improvised, and the actors who must breathe life into them, have strong emotional sides to their natures. In attempting to manipulate the actors as his pawns (or marionettes), Hinkfuss fails to make the leap to the *sentimento* apprehension of life. Since the actors and characters live at this level, a conflict arises and action must be taken.

As soon as Hinkfuss is expelled, the actors prepare for the final scene, which shows Mommina's relationship with Rico Verri, whom she married after her father's death. The Leading Actress wants the scenery for her big moment, the room that has become a jail for her. The others suggest that the physical reality of her confinement will be created if she believes in it strongly enough. Then, under the leadership of the Character Actress, in the role of her mother, they begin to transform Mommina from the way she looks now (right after her father's death) to her appearance after several years of marriage. A mirror is called for so that she can apply the proper makeup. This scene is a mirror of the earlier

Sampognetta scene. We are watching the transformational quality of the theater: the ability of an actor to become someone else. With Sampognetta there were the two levels of the old actor and his character; here there are three levels: the Leading Actress, Mommina before marriage, and Mommina after marriage. The constant change and multiplicity of the personality articulated in seemingly abstract terms by the Father in *Six Characters* has now found complete dramatic expression, as the audience watches the transformation of both actress and character.

While the Leading Actress is being made up, the dual nature of the theater is emphasized. The actress is being aided by her sister actresses, yet as the scene progresses the theatrical reality takes over, just as it did with Sampognetta. After most of the makeup has been applied, it is the character Nenè who tells her sister Mommina to look in the mirror she is holding. Mommina refuses, saying:

> No! He has taken away all the mirrors from the house. Do you know where I can still look? In windows, like a ghost, or disfigured in the ripple of the water in the washbasin—and I remain startled at the sight.

The awful physical and emotional effects of aging and misery are graphically presented through the transformation of makeup and acting, a theatrical transformation that of course mirrors the similar process in life. The connection between art and life is made through the Leading Actress, who assumes her character and does not break from it. Although the appearances of the scene suggest the falsity of theatrical makeup, its reality is the opposite: for Mommina the gray hair and wrinkles are not make-believe but real.

After she has been made up, the Leading Actress creates the reality of her home-prison by saying, "This is wall—This is wall—This is wall," as she delineates the theatrical space that will become her character's reality. The Character Actress presents the necessary background material, speaking *"as if she were reading out of a book,"* and then Mommina is ready for her confrontation with her husband, Rico. Verri has imprisoned his wife in their home out of extreme jealousy but is still not satisfied. He wants to be able to know and control her thoughts and even her dreams. He fears she has another man—though only in her memory—and is also jealous of her past and her family. Rico is a pathological figure, yet his psychological makeup is one common to Italian men. Once again Pirandello has taken care to base his scene and character in reality, even if the image he creates is somewhat exaggerated. On another level, moreover, Verri represents the distortion of perception and interpretation that is one of Pirandello's favorite themes. Verri sees Mommina in a certain way, and nothing can convince him that her reality may be something very different.

The confrontation between Rico and Mommina and the subsequent moments in which Mommina is left alone, encounters her sisters, and finally dies trying to sing the aria from Giuseppe Verdi's *Il Trovatore* she had performed earlier are in fact some of the most realistic scenes Pirandello ever wrote. That they occur as the climax to one of his most experimental plays—constantly shifting between actor reality and stage reality and using the technique of improvisation as its basis—is not accidental. As with the Sampognetta scene, Pirandello is exploring not only the reality of life, no matter how melodramatic it might be, but also the ease with which theatrical reality can be created and made believable. If the line between illusion and reality is tenuous and often indistinguishable in life (as the previous plays argue), then the same holds true in the theater, the mirror image of life.

In order to strengthen this connection between art and life, the end of *Tonight We Improvise* reiterates the performance-in-life motif that had been developed previously. Although earlier the theatrical world of opera had been a metaphorical escape for the La Croce family, there was also the hope that it would provide a real escape as well. A successful opera career for one of her daughters would liberate Ignazia and her family from the impoverished pettiness and lack of culture of the small town she hated so vehemently. As Mommina tells her children, she should have been the sister to have made the career, but instead she married Rico and Totina became the diva. The contrast between the world of Mommina's past dreams as opposed to her present physical reality is yet another way that Pirandello suggests the manifold nature of what is commonly identified as "the truth."

Verri has completely isolated his wife from the outside world.

His disgust at Mommina's performing for other people (including her own family) has resulted in a jealousy that includes her past as well as the possibility of other men in the present. When he leaves her alone, Totina and the rest of her family pay a brief visit. After they depart, Mommina tries to explain to her children what a theater is and what opera is. She wants to demonstrate the talent she had in the past, but she has lost her ability to sing. While she explains the plot of *Il Trovatore* and tries to recapture the past by singing one of its arias, she is dying, the unaccustomed activity putting strain on her weak heart.

Il Trovatore deals with the revenge of a Gypsy woman, Azucena (the part Mommina once sang), who had unwittingly killed her own son years before. She gains her revenge on the duke responsible for her son's death by arranging for him to kill his own brother, whom everyone else believes to be Azucena's son. Pirandello uses the audience's assumed familiarity with the opera not only to create levels of reality (the opera within a play within a play) but also to create levels of melodrama. The plot of *Il Trovatore* is melodramatic, and so is the scene that Mommina is playing. The reality of Mommina's scene is established, however, not only by the commitment made by the actress (something that will be reinforced shortly), but also by the comparison with the less realistic melodrama of the Azucena aria Mommina tries to sing for her children. On the surface, Mommina's scene may appear to be obviously exaggerated and unreal. Yet Pirandello uses all possible devices to establish its reality, just as he has done with *Tonight We Improvise* itself, climaxing a play of obvious theatricality with this moment of stage "realism."

The use of *umorismo* is intentionally complex here. Pirandello has moved beyond the paradoxes of the reality of the fictional constructs called characters, and beyond the need to prove to his audience that surfaces can be intentionally misleading. In *Tonight We Improvise* he keeps his audience off balance with frequent changes of perspective. As soon as the reality of one level has been established, he shifts out of it, suggesting that it may not have been all that it appeared to be, or what really is of prime importance. He adds the performance aspects of life, particularly the operatic, to extend the interpenetration of art and life even further, and to present a melodramatic contrast to the final scene that allows it to appear more realistic by comparison.

Despite the fact that we have watched Mommina make herself up for the final scene and have been reminded throughout the evening that the play being improvised for us is not real, the final scene does come alive as the real suffering and death of Mommina. Her confrontations with her jealous husband and with the family whose success she should have not only shared but been responsible for have driven her to the desperation of the final moments. She has been abandoned by everyone but her children and needs to communicate to them the reality of her past, which of course has now become nothing but a memory. The point about a person passing through a series of personalities, suggested first in Mommina's making up, is dramatized more fully here as we see her metamorphosed, frantically trying to convince both her children and herself of the reality of the person she was in the past. She can create the picture of the theater in her imagination and in words, but she fails when she tries to actually become the performer she once was.

As she tries to escape from her wretched present by recapturing the Mommina of the past, she is only drawn to the episode that made the present moment inevitable. She tries to sing Azucena's aria, but instead of being drawn into the reality of *Il Trovatore* and her character, she remembers that this is the very aria she sang the night her father returned to the house and died, the same night her destiny was sealed. Whether she married Rico out of gratitude (as she interprets the character) or out of desperation (as Hinkfuss sees it), the result is the same. She has lost her voice, her youth, her beauty, and most important, her freedom. She dies singing a farewell, the old Gypsy woman's farewell to another character and her own farewell to life.

The reaction of Verri and the La Croce women to Mommina's death has barely begun when Dr. Hinkfuss interrupts them, running through the auditorium and screaming "magnificent, magnificent!" as he congratulates them for delivering what he wanted. Hinkfuss now reveals that he has never left the theater, that he was with the lighting designer helping create the lighting effects for the scene. Pirandello mentions these effects in directions for various stages in Mommina's scene, and it is clear that they contributed to the reality of those moments. The actors had wanted to create their characters completely on their own but had not done so. The artifice has become intertwined with the reality. Although Totina says that she suspected the use of the lighting effects, the acting and lighting have come together so well that during the actual performance the reality of the characters in their environment has been the only concern. And yet that reality was of course merely the pretense of art, even if it did convince an audience of the truth of the emotions being expressed.

The arrival of Hinkfuss jolts the audience back into the realization that what they had just seen was a fiction being created by a group of actors. He spoils the audience's pleasure in their involvement in the reality of Mommina's scene and the actors' pleasure in their accomplishment. A possible reality to that fiction is then suggested when one of the actors sees the Leading Actress lying on the ground, in the position she assumed for Mommina's death. Pirandello suggests the possiblity of the actual death of the Leading Actress, and thus the coincidence of the two levels of reality, only momentarily. She has fainted because of her excessive involvement with her character. As the old Comic Actor says, improvisation is too dangerous and involves risks that a fixed script does not offer. Hinkfuss agrees to use a script, but not one provided by a playwright. He wants the life that only can be supplied by actors creating their own characters. No real resolution is reached, however, since both the insights into life and the dangers inherent in such close identification of actor and character have been explored by the play.

Tonight We Improvise ends more ambiguously than the other two theater trilogy plays. Pirandello uses this ambiguity as part of his dramatic statement as well as technique. The theater—the hall of mirrors that not only reflects life but also gives it some of its basic images—can be an artifice that shows the audience certain insights into life while remaining separate and clearly discernible from it. As life becomes more fragmented, and as the need to move from an *avvertimento* reaction to the surface, the way things appear, to the *sentimento* response to the reality underneath becomes more crucial, and more difficult, the theater reflecting that life must change accordingly.

One way the theater can change is by opening up the manner in which it presents its stories. At the core of each of the theater trilogy plays lies a set of characters and a conflict that could easily be treated in realistic terms. Instead, Pirandello acknowledges that he is dramatizing these situations in the theater, using actors to portray characters. The relationships between the actors and characters and between the play being produced and the audience are thus made more complex. The audience's feeling of security, of knowing what kind of play it is seeing, is threatened. In challenging the reality of the characters of his fictions by juxtaposing their reality with that of the actors charged with bringing them to life, he finds a dramatic metaphor for the ideas he wants to express. In the same way, he has found in *umorismo* a dramatic premise that both embodies his ideas and suggests a way of bringing them to life.

By now the idea that illusion and reality can become so intertwined as to be indistinguishable from each other may seem trite. The same is true for the multiplicity of the personality and the difficulty of really "knowing" either another human being or "the truth." Yet these ideas, when they are abstractions spouted either by characters in the plays or critics analyzing them, lie on the surface of Pirandello's work. By themselves these abstractions only confuse the real issue in Pirandello: how the ideas affect the people who are influenced by them. As abstractions they lead only to reckless curiosity and the increase of suffering.

Tonight We Improvise concludes Pirandello's exploration of the relationship between life and the theater that mirrors it by showing their mutual dependence on each other. Although there is much interpenetration between the two, a distinction must ultimately remain. There must be a Dr. Hinkfuss arranging the lighting effects. There must not be complete identification between actor and role, between illusion and reality. Beneath the *avvertimento* surface of this play—where it appears that theater has become life, and life theater—there is the felt realization that life itself is possible only because certain distinctions can be made. These distinctions may be established with great difficulty and may be only partial, but they are necessary in order to keep life under control.

The final vision toward which the play moves is a compromise, a synthesis of two opposing approaches. Neither the actors nor Hinkfuss has a monopoly on the truth; in fact, it lies somewhere between their two extreme positions. As Pirandello has advocated from the first publication of *L'umorismo* in 1908, both intellect and emotion must contribute to perception and judgment.

The conflict between thought and passion that is embodied in the opposition of the director and his troupe of actors is intensified by their ethnic identification. By means of a German director and Sicilian characters, Pirandello employs the traditional stereotypes of the cold, intellectual northern Europeans and the hot, passionate southerners. As with many stereotypes, however, they do contain some basic truth. The order and discipline of Hinkfuss and the spontaneity and passion of the actor-characters are both necessary if the play is to take shape.[9]

Although Giudice is correct in his analysis of Tilgher's flux-form dichotomy and the tyranny it exerted over some of Pirandello's late plays, the theater trilogy plays, as extensions of earlier work, are exceptions. *Tonight We Improvise* is the logical conclusion of the thematic and dramaturgic explorations that began in *Six Characters*. Although *Each in His Own Way* and *Tonight We Improvise* both use the flux-and-form image more self-consciously than *Six Characters*, they ultimately affirm the synthesis advocated by the *sentimento del contrario* rather than the opposition of life with fictions seeking to delimit and stagnate it. The flux-form dichotomy is certainly stated overtly in *L'umorismo;* Tilgher's decision to make it the key to Pirandello's drama gave it a predominance not found in the essay. As *Tonight We Improvise* illustrates, even late in his career Pirandello created opposition and conflict in order to suggest the need for moderation rather than extremism.

In *The Theatre of Revolt*, Brustein attacks Pirandello for not having the courage of his convictions, for proceeding only partway with his theatrical experimentation:

> Pirandello is unable to dispense with stage illusion, despite his angry attacks on it. The actors in the theatre trilogy are no longer pretending to be characters, but they are pretending to be actors—actors created in the imagination of Pirandello. And though the stage is now strictly a stage, it is still, to some extent, an illusionistic stage. In *Six Characters,* for example, the action takes place during a rehearsal in an empty theatre, but the rehearsal is really a performance, the "empty theatre" filled with paying spectators. Actually, whatever spontaneity occurs in these theatre plays is carefully planned by the author. As is often the case in these matters, Pirandello has destroyed one convention—and substituted another.... Thus, Pirandello has not destroyed illusions; he has merely multi-

plied illusions. Contemptuous of imitation, he is unable to do without it. In his experimental drama, theory and practice fail to merge; idea and action fail to occur.[10]

Although it is true that *Six Characters* is not really a rehearsal, *Each in His Own Way* a *commedia a chiave*, or *Tonight We Improvise* an improvised play, they are suitable incarnations of Pirandello's ideas. He may have substituted one kind of illusion for another, but the illusion he creates at least acknowledges its theatrical identity. More important, it is an illusion that is so constructed as to lead the perceptive audience member to an apprehension of the reality underneath. Pirandello is not contemptuous of art as the imitation of life; he is contemptuous of art as the imitation of other art. By viewing the theater process in a forthright and original manner, he suggests the need for a complex way of seeing that probes beneath the surface. In the same way he shows that one can learn about life not only by observing the reflections it gives off but also by examining the mirror that sends back those reflected images.

At the same time, however, he realizes that for his audience some illusion, some realistic connection, is still necessary. Just as Pirandello views compromise and synthesis as essential to life, so he extends this belief into his theater practice. He is not an anarchist like the Futurists; there is a need to replace old structures with new, more responsive ones. To that end the theater trilogy, and perhaps especially *Tonight We Improvise*, demonstrates not the failure of Pirandello's theory and practice, but its triumph: the emergence of an innovative dramatic form that reflects the ideas of multiplicity and tolerance held by its creator.

6.

Enrico IV (1922)

The three plays of the theater trilogy may well constitute Pirandello's most original accomplishment, an exploration of the relationship between theater art and life that had neither been attempted previously nor has been duplicated since. Yet despite the achievement of these plays, taken either as separate works or as a trilogy, another play, written after *Six Characters* but before the other two, may be his masterpiece. This play, *Enrico IV (Henry IV)*, is not a theater play in the same literal sense that the trilogy plays are. Yet it uses almost every aspect of theatrical art, not only to express its ideas with the full resources of the medium, but to further explore the theme of the theatricalization of life that is one of the focal points of the trilogy. The very fact that *Enrico IV* maintains an "illusionistic frame" while dissecting the way in which its central character interacts with history, the other characters, and his own special kind of theater may indeed have allowed Pirandello a freedom of breadth and depth that enables this play to equal and even surpass the insights and stunning theatricality of the trilogy.

The intriguing complexity of the ideas Pirandello deals with in

Enrico IV, and the closeness of the subject of madness to his own tragic life,[1] may explain the fascination these ideas have had for most critics. And themes such as the reality or illusory quality of Enrico's madness, the interaction of the many levels of time, the clash between the world that Enrico has created for himself and the outsiders who attempt to destroy it and Enrico's identity as an actor are all of course central to an understanding of the play.

Many of the interpretations that investigate these ideas, however, illustrate the tendency to fix almost exclusively on the ideas themselves, without devoting enough attention to the ways in which the themes are expressed. This transcends the distinction between form and content. The themes of this play are not merely encapsulated in the theatrical metaphors structuring the play; they are strongly molded by them. *Enrico IV* is a play about madness, time, aging, masks, and the attempt to escape from one reality and substitute another of one's own making. In this substitution we see a man attempt to control his life in the same way that a playwright shapes his play or an actor his character. Enrico alternates between playing his character by choice and by accident, and this movement between the two states forms the basic rhythm of the play.

In his identification of Enrico as an actor playing a series of roles to perfection, Brustein makes an important recognition of the way Pirandello proceeds in this play.[2] It is incomplete, however, both in the way Brustein uses it and in the limits of its formulation. Not just acting, but almost every aspect of theatrical art is used as a means of establishing the world of the play and commenting on that world. Scenery, costume, and makeup become essential tools both for Enrico in the creation of his performance and for Pirandello in the creation of his play. The difficulty of establishing what reality is and what theatrical illusion in the theater itself is has now been superseded by the difficulty of making such distinctions in the world outside the theater, a world that has now adopted many of the theater's basic techniques. What is more of an illusion (a play not identifying itself as play) now curiously becomes less of one, since that illusionary life on stage is representing a theatrical performance that is intended, not as theater, but as life.

On the most elemental level, *Enrico IV* is predicated on the situation of a man costuming himself in order to play the role of another character, in this case a historical figure in a costumed cavalcade, and by accident being trapped into assuming that role as his only reality. It is important that we never learn the name of "Enrico" before the accident. Even after the revelation is made that he has known for the past six years that he is not the "real" Enrico IV, it still remains his sole identity. The role has come to dominate the actor, robbing him of everything, including his name. Thus, his theatrical milieu, created through scenery, costume, and makeup, not only creates environment but defines him as well.

Although *Enrico IV* is not a play that takes place on a stage, its action does occur within scenery specially constructed for the leading actor. After the accident forced Enrico into the belief that he was really the German king, his family tried to accommodate him. They constructed a throne room where he could play the role that had become his only reality. The counselors hired to accompany Enrico in his "masquerade" explain that the room can have various locations: Goslar, the Hartz castle, Wurms. Like many other aspects of this play, the throne room is not real but a theatrical illusion that has been built to facilitate the performance of its chief player and can be transformed from one place to another by the imagination of that player. The performance at first appears to be real, but is later revealed to be play, artifice, even though Enrico has continued his role of the king, not out of frivolity or perversity, but out of terror at returning to a world from which he was excluded for many years.

The throne room serves as the location of Enrico's performance. It is built to give the illusion of the twelfth century, even though it has such conveniences of the twentieth century as electric lights. In the midst of this room are two scenic pieces that not only reinforce the difference between medieval and modern but summarize many of the play's central themes. These pieces are two modern paintings of a man and a woman dressed in costumes of twelfth-century Germany. They portray Enrico and Matilda, the woman he loved at the time of the accident, done at the time of the masquerade, eighteen years ago. Throughout Enrico's years of playing the German king, first by chance and then by choice, they have served as a reminder of his past. Whether he believes himself to be Enrico IV or not, he is faced with the image of himself as he was eighteen years ago. In fact, as he later explains, the existence of that picture influenced his decision to remain as Enrico even after he recovered his memory. Suddenly the picture reminded him of what he looked like twelve years ago and led him to the realization that he had lost those twelve years. He had ceased to exist as himself, while his entire world, as well as all the people he knew before the accident, had experienced twelve years of life that had been denied and were unknown to him.

The companion picture of Matilda also has great significance. Enrico has been forced to live with the image of the woman he loved, yet who did not reciprocate his affection. For the first twelve years, the picture was, for him, Matilda of Tuscany, the archenemy of Enrico the king; but for the past six it has been the Marchesa Matilda Spina, the woman he loved and by whom he had been rejected before the accident, the woman who certainly would not be receptive to a renewal of that love after eighteen years. The final action of Enrico's sudden lunge for Frida, Matilda's daughter, who resembles her mother as she appears in the picture, may seem, on the surface, to be overly melodramatic. Yet Enrico's realization of the loss of his youth, compounded by the physical presence of the woman in the picture, makes his action psychologically valid.

The existence of the pictures, which are meant to dominate the play's setting, also suggests to Dr. Genoni, who has been summoned to cure Enrico, the nature of the treatment he employs to effect such a cure. The Doctor believes that the shock of seeing Frida, who is the mirror image of her mother as painted eighteen years ago, will allow Enrico to regain his lost sanity. The Doctor is sure of his plan, even though Tito Belcredi, Matilda's current lover, reminds him that Enrico must make two temporal transitions. One of these consists of the eighteen years of his illness, while the other is the eight-hundred-year chasm between the twelfth and twentieth centuries. The Doctor cites the resiliency of the human being as the source of his confidence in the advisability of his plan and thus acts to put it into effect.

The Doctor's ignorance, as well as the shallowness of his thinking, is stressed throughout. He compares Enrico to a clock and constantly uses dehumanizing medical jargon. The Doctor's plan is to have Frida, dressed as her mother, and Carlo, Enrico's nephew and Frida's fiancé, take the place of the two pictures in the niches of the throne room. When Enrico sees the youthful images of himself and Matilda brought to life, he will be shocked back into reality. As Enrico later explains, however, the Doctor has neglected to take into consideration the crucial effect that seeing pictures come to life might have. Enrico may be mad in the sense that he thinks he is the German emperor, but at least he can function within his reality and is not dangerous to his associates or himself.[3] The fright of seeing paintings come to life might well worsen his insanity rather than cure it. Enrico has suffered greatly and has tried to cope with that suffering as well as he possibly can. The Doctor sees him only as a case, a puzzle to be solved, a watch to be repaired, and as a result he uses the scenic elements of the paintings to force Enrico into a situation that leads to his entrapment rather than to his liberation.

Both the masquerade that Enrico has been part of since his fall and the cure that Dr. Genoni hopes will dislodge him from his madness also depend heavily on the use of costume. The original cavalcade, the scene of the accident eighteen years ago, was a costume party, with each participant choosing a historical personage and dressing in imitation of him or her. When Matilda chose to dress as Matilda of Tuscany because of the similarity of name, the man who loved her but whom she rejected chose to be Enrico IV, the king betrayed to his mortal enemy the pope by the historical Matilda. When Enrico fell off his horse and really believed himself to be the German emperor, his entire life became a costume party, with all the people around him forced to dress in costume and play the roles of historical characters with whom the original Enrico had interacted.

After the visitors decide to meet with Enrico, the counselors emphasize the need for them all to don costumes. If Enrico should see people in unfamiliar garb, the shock, they believe, would not jolt him back into the present but would send him into a rage, convinced that the unsuitable clothes constituted part of an act of witchcraft perpetrated by his enemy, the pope. As the counselors dress Matilda, Belcredi, and the Doctor for their presentation before Enrico, they emphasize that the costume, and not the person wearing it, is what matters. Different people often appear before Enrico in the same costume, as the same historical figure, since he notices the clothes and not the person beneath them. In a society so concerned with trivial values, it is natural that such an assumption should be made. Yet Enrico, both before the accident and now, has never been such a man. He plunges beneath the *avvertimento* level to the *sentimento,* and in so doing often experiences great pain. It thus may appear, at first, that his decision to remain as Enrico even after his awakening might be caused by a desire to remain in a world of appearances, of costume and mask. It is, however, his keen awareness of the superficiality of the real world and the suffering his reemergence into that world would cause that lead to his continuation of the role and his preference for the costume world of Enrico IV.

If costume is a crucial part of the Doctor's plan to force Enrico's return to the twentieth century, it is also part of Pirandello's technique of creating a sense of dislocation in his audience. From the first scene introducing the new counselor, Bertoldo, who is dressed in the costume of a time and country different from that of the other three advisers because he thought he was to be involved in the world of Henri IV of France, there is a sense of confusion created by the play. This ambiguity is heightened when the arrival of the entourage headed by Carlo and Matilda is announced by Giovanni, the old family retainer, who is dressed in contemporary evening clothes. When Matilda and the others enter in their modern dress, the conflict between past and present is communicated in strikingly visual terms. Throughout *Enrico IV* characters are constantly changing clothes and in so doing move from one historical period to another. Although they do not know it at the time, they are all being manipulated by Enrico, who is continuing as performance something that began as masquerade and then became a reality. Now that it both is and is not his reality, the continuation of his role as Enrico IV means that everyone who wants to have contact with him must enter his world and play the game of life under his rules and conditions.

The uneasiness generated by this costume game can be seen in Frida's reaction to the role assigned her. She is a pawn in the plan engineered by the Doctor, with the assistance of her mother and her fiancé, to shock Enrico back to "normalcy." Although she feels uncomfortable in the costume, which gives her a frightening resemblance to her mother's picture, she is like the others in her blindness to the danger and folly of the Doctor's cure. Frida lacks sufficient sophistication to ponder either the possible trauma Enrico might experience upon seeing paintings spring to life or the adjustments he would have to make after eighteen years in "exile." Yet the unfamiliarity of the costume itself and the image with which it identifies her cause an inquietude that hints at the risks involved in her masquerade. If the audience remains oblivious to these perils, then they stand to be trapped by the play's conclusion in the same way the intruders do.

The use of costume in *Enrico IV* thus reinforces one of Pirandello's favorite themes: the fragmentation and uncertainty of contemporary life. The scenery can place location at Goslar, Worms, or the Hartz castle. Costume can reveal the time as the twelfth or twentieth century, or a bizarre combination of the two. In fact, Enrico lives in a no-man's-land that is neither medieval nor modern but is poised between them. He can no longer believe himself to be the real Enrico, as he did for the first twelve years following the accident. On the other hand, he cannot return to a contemporary existence for fear of being even more of an outsider than he was previously. This inability to cope with a hopelessly fragmented world forces Enrico to choose the masks and illusions of the theater, seeking refuge in the only realm in which he can exercise some semblance of control.

As important as scenery and costume are to the substantiation of *Enrico IV*, makeup is probably the most important visual theatrical device used in the play. It is the key to the physical transformation of actor into character in the theater, and since Pirandello's plays ultimately focus on the characters themselves, sometimes as actors and other times not, it is logical that makeup be granted a central position here. From the grotesquely made up old woman who triggers the process of *L'umorismo* to the dual transformation in *Tonight We Improvise*—that of the Leading Actress and younger version of her character, Mommina, into the older Mommina—Pirandello shows a fascination with the art of makeup as the means of creating a new image of oneself. In *Enrico IV*, a work that lies chronologically between the early essay and late play, the makeup of Enrico and Matilda establishes key aspects of their characters and their relationship.

Pirandello stresses the makeup they are wearing, as characters and not as actors, in the descriptions of both Matilda and Enrico, Matilda is described as follows:

around forty-five years old; still beautiful and shapely, but with too much evidence of measures taken against the inevitable damages of age with a violent yet well-thought-out makeup that sharply transforms her head into that of a Valkyrie. This makeup creates a relief that contrasts with and strongly contradicts her mouth, which is very beautiful and full of anguish.

The contradictions inherent in *umorismo*, and the need to probe beneath the surface in order fully to understand someone, can be seen in this image of Matilda. She has also made herself into a theatrical, or rather operatic, figure from Richard Wagner's Ring cycle. When Enrico enters later in the act, the following image is presented:

Enrico is near fifty, very pale, and already gray at the back of his head; in contrast, at the temples and front he appears blond, through a dye job that is very obvious, almost childish. On his cheeks, in the midst of his tragic pallor, he has the red makeup of a doll that is also very obvious. He wears the penitent's sackcloth over his royal garb, as at Canossa. In his eyes there is an agonized stare that is frightening, in contrast with the costume of a person who wishes to be a humble penitent, as if the more on display he is, the greater he feels that this humiliation is undeserved.

Even before he speaks of the differences between the uses of makeup employed by himself and Matilda, Enrico's makeup is both a reflection and a parody of Matilda's. There is a self-consciousness in Enrico's makeup that acknowledges its ridiculousness, while Matilda's seems to have been done in earnest, even if the result is grotesque and inadvertently theatrical.

In his first appearance, garbed in his penitent's robes, Enrico analyzes the makeup he and Matilda are wearing and the relationship of that makeup to age. Just as age was central to the old lady's use of makeup in *L'umorismo* (to keep her younger husband) and to Mommina's transformation, here it motivates the creation of a younger image, an image that will appear real even if it is not. Enrico sees a crucial distinction, however, in the ways the two of them use makeup. He has been speaking of how each person has his own vision of himself, and how the individual maintains this vision, even if life changes it:

But all of us continue to hold tightly to our own concepts of ourselves, even to the extent that some who are growing old dye their hair. What difference does it make that my dye job cannot possibly be, for any of you, the real color of my hair. You, Madonna, you certainly do not do it to deceive others, or even yourself; but only to fool, a very little bit, your image in front of the mirror. I do it for fun. You do it seriously. But I assure you that no matter how serious you are, even you are part of a masquerade, Madonna. I'm not talking about the venerable crown that surrounds your brow, and which I kneel to, or your ducal mantle. I mean only that memory which you want to artificially fix of yourself when you were blond, on a day that pleased you; or of your darker color if you were a brunette: the image of your youth that has now faded....

The audience, as well as the other characters, are not yet aware that Enrico is cured, that he knows he is not the real Enrico IV and is consciously playing the role. His words to Matilda have a sting, however, that does not seem appropriate for the historical role Matilda is playing, that of Adelaide, the mother of Enrico's wife. Adelaide has assisted Enrico, so that the sharpness with which he penetrates through her masquerade suggests an awareness on Enrico's part that Matilda perceives but that the Doctor rejects.[4] Beneath the surface level of historical role playing and Enrico's realization of the histrionics of others while they are unaware of his, however, lies the more important aspect of the role playing of ages. Whether as Enrico and Adelaide or as the man who became Enrico and Matilda, they are still middle-aged people wearing makeup and hair dye in order to appear younger than they are.

Just as he is more fully aware of the various levels of the historical masquerade, Enrico also has more insight into the masquerade of age. Matilda's makeup is motivated by vanity, an attempt to cheat the mirror image of herself she must face every day. She takes this image more seriously than Enrico does, and yet it becomes less important for her than for him. He has considered the implications of such makeup more and has probed beneath the surface to realize the impossibility of making such a mask real. His perception of the ridiculousness of his makeup and its necessary failure make him suffer over the loss of youth in a way that

Matilda does not. More important, however, is Enrico's need to recapture his youth. Matilda may dread the ravages of time, but at least she has fully experienced the passage of that time. Enrico has lost eighteen years, including the twelve stolen from him by the accident. In a sense, he went to sleep when he was still young and awoke as a middle-aged man, having been "exiled" from twelve years of prime life enjoyed by everyone else. He has progressed twelve years on the journey toward death without having experienced the stops along the way.

Using a technique similar to that of the old lady described in *L'umorismo,* Enrico appears to be a ridiculous clown when he first enters. Even though he is the victim of a cruel twist of fortune, his sackcloth and makeup suggest a man who has become a "joke of the gods." It is only through the exploration of Enrico's character, beginning with his speech on makeup, that another response becomes necessary. As Enrico shares with us his realization that he is not the real Enrico IV, and more important, the reasons why he chose to remain hidden behind the historical mask, and as we learn more about the people he would have to deal with if he reentered the twentieth century, our assessment of him alters. The *avvertimento* response to Enrico's surface, which includes the objectivity necessary to comedy, is superseded by the *sentimento* response to the reality underneath, causing a sympathetic understanding of the man that makes laughter impossible.

The visual aspects of *Enrico IV* establish the theatrical milieu within which Enrico plays his life; even more important, they create the various time levels of the play. *Enrico IV* is a play about the process of time, its relativity, and its constant and unstoppable passing. It is also about a man's most critical experience of time's passage—aging. The process of growing old—of becoming a series of other persons, physically as well as psychologically, of remembering what one once looked and acted like—is dealt with graphically. The fixity of one's image in the past (as represented concretely by the paintings of Enrico and Matilda) is contrasted with the change of image in the present, including the use of makeup in a futile attempt to stop the change of time and make life conform to the image of the past.

In the theater trilogy, Pirandello juxtaposed the ongoing passage of life with the fixity of art. Here it is the fixity of the past, of history, that is held up against the flow of life. Both history on a large scale (the German Empire of the twelfth century) and on a personal level (Enrico as he was eighteen years ago) are contrasted with life as it is proceeding in the now of the play. The costumes and scenery establish the twelfth-century masquerade of the past that is both trap and refuge for Enrico, while the makeup serves primarily as an attempt to bridge the smaller but more crucial chasm over the eighteen years that have passed between the accident and the present. As makeup helps establish, the question of Enrico's madness or sanity becomes much less important than his attempts to deal with time and aging and the years that have been irrevocably lost to him.

Although the visual images of this play are significant, the essence of *Enrico IV* must be sought in the theatrical metaphor that identifies Enrico as an actor, director, and playwright. Although he is primarily an actor, Enrico not only conceives and executes his own role but directs others in a scenario of his own invention. After he reveals his sanity to his counselors, he chides them because they have been living his dream, his madness. They have been puppets, manipulated both by the family that hired them and the man they serve. Enrico at least first believed in the drama he was enacting, and then sought refuge in it. They, on the other hand, are merely hired hands who do not even understand the nature of the drama they are asked to perform.

Enrico's attempt to control his life during the past six years, when he has known that he was not really Enrico IV, has been a form of artistic creation. As actor, director, and even playwright, he has sought to sustain a reality that was once real but is now illusory. Reality has become theater for Enrico, just as theater (in the form of the masquerade where he chose to play Enrico in order to be close to Matilda) became reality through the accident. As actor he has been at the center of the drama, but as director and conceiver he has shaped not only his own performance but that of those around him as well. Even after he reveals himself to the counselors, he still acts as director when they want to make fun of Giovanni, who is still unaware of Enrico's sanity. Enrico forbids them to make sport of the old man and resumes his role of emperor so that Giovanni can continue his loyal service to him.

It is difficult to isolate the aspects of Enrico as director and author because he is essentially an actor, and his directing and conception spring from this source. Although he is an actor in his performance as the German emperor and, as Brustein point out, is an old emperor enacting the part of a young emperor,[5] it is crucial to understand that Enrico has not become an actor only because of the accident. Dressing up for a costume party does not make him an actor, nor does the accident that makes that role real to him. After he has reawakened into the twentieth century, he decides to continue playing the role as a conscious creation. Yet even before the accident he was an actor. While his decision to continue playing Enrico IV can be seen as having been influenced by the twelve years he has lost, it is also shaped by the kind of man he was before he fell.

The information about Enrico's identity as an actor before the accident is revealed by Matilda and Tito in Act I. Matilda, in fact, says that she made him into an actor even when he did not intend to be one. Enrico tried to convince Matilda of the authenticity of his love for her and became an earnest suitor toward her. She could not take him, or any other man in this position, seriously. She viewed his wooing as a performance, whereas he did not. The urgency of his love was both comical and frightening to her, so she mocked the sincere proferring of that love and turned it into a performance, at least insofar as she received it as audience, even if it was not intended that way by him as "actor."

It is Matilda's current lover, Tito Belcredi, who offers the real clue to Enrico's personality before the accident and to his identity as "actor" even then. After Matilda has described Enrico's attempts at courting her, the Doctor tries to get a clearer picture of "Enrico's" original personality:

DOCTOR: Then, it seems that even at that time he was somewhat of a fanatic, if I understand what you are saying.
BELCREDI: Yes, but in a very curious way, Doctor.
DOCTOR: How would that be?
BELCREDI: Well, I would say he acted ... coldly.
MATILDA: What are you talking about, coldly? It was like this, Doctor, he was a bit strange, certainly, but full of life, extraverted.
BELCREDI: I'm not saying the he simulated his exultation. In fact,

to the contrary, he was often genuinely excited. But I could swear, Doctor, that he would suddenly see himself in the midst of his own exultation. And I believe that this must have happened to him during every spontaneous action he ever made. I'll go even further: I am certain that he suffered because of this self-vision. There were times when he had the most comic fits of anger against himself.

MATILDA: This is true.

BELCREDI *(to Donna Matilda):* But why? *(to the Doctor)* In my opinion it was because the sudden realization that he was giving a performance put him at odds against all intimacy with his own feelings, which then seemed to him—not false, because he was sincere—but like something that must immediately be validated, how shall I put it ... by an act of intelligence that would substitute for the cordiality and sincerity he felt he lacked. Thus he improvised, exaggerated, let himself go for this very reason: to dull his senses and not watch himself any further. He seemed unsteady, fatuous, and ... yes, one has to say even ridiculous at times.

Tito has difficulty in presenting an exact description of Enrico's behavior, and the motivation behind that behavior, because he is trying to come to terms with a strange phenomenon. Enrico seemed to watch his own actions at the moment he was discharging them, thus becoming not only performer but audience as well.

With Enrico, Pirandello has created a character who has always been at odds, not only with the world around him and the people who inhabit it, but with himself and his own actions as well. Because he can draw back and watch his actions as he performs them, Enrico becomes alienated from these actions, but more important, he becomes alienated also from his own emotions, which seem suspect to him through the objective stance he assumes toward himself. He is also convinced that others must view those acts as he does, as part of a performance, and thus he compensates with improvisations and other devices in an attempt to narrow the gap between what he really feels and what is regarded as show by making all his acts into theater. The opposite result is achieved, however, and he becomes alienated even more from others and himself.

The dual nature of the human personality is a phenomenon that Pirandello had pondered for many years; perhaps it is the reason he ultimately chose the theater and its schizophrenic division between actor and role as his principal medium of expression. Before he was married to Antonietta, he wrote to her of the two sides to his own nature:

> There are almost two people within me. You already know one of them; not even I know the other one very well. I could say that I'm composed of a big me and a little me, with these two gentlemen almost always at war against each other, the one often totally antipathetic toward the other. The former is taciturn and continually lost in thought; the latter speaks with ease, makes jokes and isn't adverse to laughing and making others laugh.... I am perpetually divided between these two persons. Now one rules, then the other. I gravitate most naturally to the first, that is, the big me. But I sympathize with and am suited to the latter, who is, at heart, a being like everyone else, with normal desires and defects.
> Which of the two will you love the most, my Antonietta?
> Your answer will determine, to a large extent, the secret of our happiness.[6]

The question of identity is central to much of Pirandello's work, from the basic factual question of whether Signora Ponza is really Ponza's wife or Signora Frola's daughter to the more metaphysical speculation provoked by the theater trilogy and this play. His own personal problems of identity took many forms, only one of which was the introvert/extravert dichotomy mentioned above.

Pirandello's main crisis of identity, of course, originated in his wife's madness and the distorted vision of him generated by her illness. It is interesting to note that *Enrico IV* marks the last play of Pirandello's to deal with the subject of madness. It did not, unfortunately, mean that he could dismiss the subject from his own life. In the summer of 1924, after Antonietta had been hospitalized for five years, Pirandello rented a house near Spoleto so that she could be with him. She refused to leave the clinic, however, and resumed treating him as her enemy. She remained in the clinic until her death, which occurred after World War II.[7]

Pirandello's professional life also brought identity problems. In order to support his family he began teaching in a girls' school in 1897 and continued to do so until 1922, the year of *Enrico IV,* when he could finally support himself as a writer. He disliked teaching, and as his writing career developed he was frequently absent from school. Even the writing caused difficulties. He was uncomfortable with literary socializing and the fame that accompanied his success. It also took him a long time to find the medium best suited to communicate his artistic vision, since he began writing short stories and novels and didn't find his identity as a playwright until his mid-forties. The acceptance of these plays, especially the more experimental ones, was not immediate. In fact, as a cruel and ironic reminder of the hardships he faced as both man and artist, he was assaulted by the audience leaving the theater after the premiere of *Six Characters* in Rome, which had precipitated a theater riot, with laughter, whistles, jeers, and comments like "insane asylum" and "that madman Pirandello."[8]

Sampognetta in *Tonight We Improvise* is Pirandello's experiment with the duality between actor and character, and the sustaining of both identities simultaneously. In this play, the duality is expressed within the same level of reality. Enrico's alienation from his own actions and emotions makes him appear to be an actor even when he does not intend it. When people then identify him as actor, he consciously chooses that role to close the gap between appearance and reality. Yet the extremity of his actions as performer only increases the alienation, first between himself and others, and then within himself. Pirandello's plays are peopled with characters who wear masks; yet when one of these characters demonstrates an awareness of this mask-wearing, he sometimes becomes a threat both to others and ultimately to himself.

Although Tito's description reveals much about Enrico and his mode of behavior prior to the accident, it also illuminates the type of society in which Enrico lived. Tito seems to perceive the suffering caused by Enrico's alienation, yet at the same time calls his fits of anger against himself "most comic" and describes Enrico's attempts to lose himself in performance as making him "unsteady, fatuous, and ... ridiculous." Even though Tito later believes in Enrico's performance as the German king more than Matilda, who insists that Enrico recognizes her, he appears to have studied Enrico's behavior before the accident with greater intensity and insight.

Tito has devoted careful thought to his analysis of Enrico's behavior, yet this analysis is totally an intellectual one. Tito has probed beneath the surface of the actions themselves in order to search for the motivation, and he is even aware of suffering. It remains, however, an intellectual awareness of suffering, an *avvertimento,* rather than a sympathetic coming to terms with the causes and effects of Enrico's attempts to deal with life. Both Matilda and Tito have been amused and puzzled by Enrico's behavior, but they have not been moved; they have not felt the suffering that compels him to perform and yet is intensified by that very activity, an activity destined to alienate him from his emotions and his real self, whatever that self might be.

The Doctor is intrigued by Tito's analysis and solicits further information on Enrico's identity as an actor, asking first if Enrico's actions were unsociable:

BELCREDI: No, not at all. He was well known as an organizer of tableaus, dances, theater benefits. All for fun, of course. Did you know that he was a very good actor?
CARLO DI NOLLI: And with his madness he has become a magnificent and terrifying actor!
BELCREDI: But he was even before that. In fact, at the time of the accident, after he fell from the horse, we thought . . .
DOCTOR: He hit his head, didn't he?
MATILDA: Oh, it was horrible. He was next to me. I saw him between the horse's legs, as it was rearing them.
BELCREDI: But at first none of us thought that anything serious had happened. Yes, the cavalcade stopped and there was some commotion, some people wanted to see what was going on. But he had already been taken away into the villa.
MATILDA: There was nothing to see. Not even the smallest scratch, or a drop of blood.
BELCREDI: We thought he had merely fainted . . .
MATILDA: And when, around two hours later . . .
BELCREDI: He appeared in the villa's salon—that's what I have been trying to say . . .
MATILDA: Oh, what a face he had. I realized immediately.

BELCREDI: But you did not. You cannot say that. No one realized it, that's the point, Doctor.
MATILDA: That's because you were all like madmen.
BELCREDI: Everyone was playing his part as a joke. It was like the Tower of Babel.
MATILDA: You can imagine, Doctor, what terror there was when we realized that he was not joking, that he was playing his part for real.
DOCTOR: Then he was there too?
BELCREDI: Yes! He came into the middle of the room. We all thought that he was all right, and that he was acting along with the rest of us, only better, because, as I said, he was an excellent actor. In short, what a jest.
MATILDA: We began to hit him . . .
BELCREDI: And then, he was armed—as the king—he drew his sword against two or three of us. It was a terrifying moment for us all.
MATILDA: I will never forget that scene, all of our masked faces, troubled and terrified, in front of that terrible mask of his, that was no longer a mask, but Madness.
BELCREDI: Enrico IV, Enrico IV himself, in person, in a moment of fury.
MATILDA: He was acting the obsession of that mask, Doctor, an obsession that had been overpowering him for more than a month. He always dedicated himself to everything he did with this kind of obsession.
BELCREDI: What study he had made in preparation! Down to the smallest details, minute points . . .
DOCTOR: That's easy to understand. What was a momentary obsession became fixed, with the fall and concussion that caused the damage to the brain. It became a fixation, perpetuating itself. He could have become an idiot, or a madman.

After having described Enrico as an actor in nontheatrical relationships, Tito completes the picture by showing how he was also an actor in the more common sense. While Enrico had made his entire life into a performance, he also staged shows that illustrated his skill in the histrionic art. Along with his ability to abstract himself from interpersonal encounters as if he were watching and commenting on his own actions, Enrico could also lose himself in the character of someone else, making his identity that of the character he was impersonating. Like all good actors, he had done extensive homework for his role as Enrico IV and was thoroughly steeped in his character when the accident occurred.

Enrico's identity as "actor" lies at the heart of this play and is usually clothed in ambiguity. Because he often seemed to be acting in his relationships prior to the fall, when the accident occurred and he continued the role of Enrico, his friends assumed that he was still participating in the masquerade, though in fact the role was now his only reality and was playing him. The description of his drawing his sword against the people who were mocking him not only foreshadows the end of the play but is a chilling example of the way distinctions between theater and reality become blurred in this play, even if the realistic frame is never broken. His friends, as "audience," were interpreting his actions in one way, while he was intending them in quite another.

When Carlo, Enrico's nephew, says that his uncle's madness has made him "a magnificent and terrifying actor," he sets the tone for the play without knowing it. The preceding exchanges have established Enrico's identity as an actor, but a crucial level is still unknown both to the other characters and to the audience. "Enrico IV" has once again become a role for him, an example of his skill as an actor, just as it was prior to the accident. In fact, he is playing Enrico IV on two levels. For those who believe he really thinks he is the emperor, his performance has one reality; for himself, as the only one who knows he is acting, thus enabling him to see through his visitors' disguises, his acting takes on a completely different reality, a reality that was lost during his twelve years of "exile."

The three-act structure of *Enrico IV* revolves around these two types of acting. In the first act Enrico appears only in his role as emperor, which everyone assumes to be his sole reality. In Act II, after a brief appearance as king, he drops his mask and reveals his realization that he is not really Enrico IV. The third act then becomes the synthesis of the first two, combining the "reality" of the prior two acts. After he kills Belcredi, Enrico will be forced to wear Enrico's mask in reality, as he did for the first twelve years, with no possibility of discarding it. Yet he will also know that Enrico is a role, a mask, as he has during the years since his awakening.

Carlo identifies his uncle's acting with madness. All the outsiders accept without question the fact that Enrico's accident has made him insane, with that insanity taking the form of his belief that he is the German king. As with much of Pirandello's work, madness is seen here in a more complex way than the attitude of Matilda, Tito, and the Doctor would suggest. If it is impossible to determine when a person is acting and when he is not, or to determine the exact nature and self-awareness he has of his performance, then the same impossibility may hold true for distinguishing madness and sanity. Is Enrico mad when he lunges at Frida and then kills Belcredi, or when he continues a masquerade that is no longer forced on him?[9]

The key issue of madness versus sanity is expressed through the opposition of Enrico and the outsiders. They of course label him as a madman. Yet can there be an absolute standard? The Doctor's plan of having paintings spring to life risks a more virulent form of madness in Enrico. Genoni's behavior may be a kind of madness itself, the madness of not taking into account either Enrico's past, as related by Tito, or the significance of the eighteen year chasm between Enrico and the rest of the twentieth-century world.

Although Enrico's madness consisted in his belief that he really was a historical figure, Pirandello is less interested in his behavior during that period than in the actions it precipitated after his recovery. Yet that past behavior must be described in detail before the central character can make his entrance. We as audience see Enrico only after his recovery, but like the others we must know of his "madness" so that the confusion between the two mental states can be established. It is in the "reality" of Enrico's behavior and his explanation for his continuation of the role of Enrico IV that the themes of acting, madness, time, and aging all come together to form the *sentimento* level of the play, a level that has been completely overlooked by the Doctor and Enrico's friends.

After Enrico has been startled by the surprise of seeing the two paintings spring to life, the Doctor, Matilda, and Tito rush in, having just learned from the counselors that he is "sane." Enrico explains that while he was "mad," everything that happened for Tito, Matilda, and everyone else did not occur for him. He awoke gradually to his real identity, considered rushing out into the world and proclaiming it, and then thought of the treatment he had received before the accident. Some people had considered him mad even before the fall, while Tito himself had been among the most ferocious of his antagonists. Enrico then begins to speak of aging:

ENRICO: And look here at my hair *(shows them the hair at the nape of his neck)*.
BELCREDI: But I have gray hair too!
ENRICO: Yes, but with this difference: that mine became gray while I was Enrico IV, do you understand? And I was not even aware of it. All of a sudden one day I opened my eyes and saw myself, and I was terrified, because I suddenly realized that not only my hair, but all of me had become gray, like this, and that everything had collapsed, that all was over, and that I would arive with the hunger of a wolf at a banquet that had already been cleared away.
BELCREDI: Eh, but the others . . .
ENRICO: *(quickly):* I know, they were eagerly awaiting my cure, even those who were behind me, and pricked my horse so that it bled . . .
CARLO: What, how's this?
ENRICO: Yes, treacherously, to make the horse rear and throw me!
MATILDA: This is the first I've heard of this!
ENRICO: It was probably done as a joke!
MATILDA: But who was it? Who was riding behind us?
ENRICO: Knowing who did it is not important. It was all those who continued to feast and who then made me eat their remnants of the meager gravy of pity, or some scrap of remorse left clinging to their dirty plate. Thank you! *(turning suddenly to the Doctor)* You see, Doctor, that you now have standing before you a case absolutely unique in the annals of insanity—I preferred to remain mad—finding everything ready here for this new kind of delight: to live—with the most lucid awareness—my own madness and to thus avenge myself on the brutality of that rock which battered my head! This solitude, which seemed so squalid and empty when I first reopened my eyes—I would cover over with all the clothes and splendors of that carnival day long ago, when you *(looks at Matilda and indicates Frida)*, there you are, Marchesa, triumphed—and I would make everyone who wished to be presented to me follow in my footsteps in that ancient

famous masquerade that had been—for you and not for me—a day's entertainment. I would make it become no longer a joke, an entertainment, but a reality, the reality of a true madness. Here all would dress in masquerade, and there would be a throne room, and my four counselors: secret, and of course traitors. *(He turns suddenly toward them.)* I would like to know what you have gained by revealing that I was cured—if I am cured, there is no more need of you, and you will be dismissed. To confide in anyone, that is truly an act of madness. Now it's my turn to accuse you. Do you know, they thought they could make fun of me in front of you. *(He breaks into laughter.)*

Enrico's image of the starving man appearing at a feast when the table has already been cleared brilliantly sums up his reason for maintaining the role of Enrico IV even after he has recovered his memory. Life has passed him by, a life that did not treat him well even when he was sane. To return to that world and be forced to accept the pity of people who had lived almost eighteen years without him would be intolerable. So he has decided to maintain the masquerade and exercise the control that would be impossible if he acknowledged his cure. All those people from his past who wanted to see him would have to accept his terms and dress as they did for the masquerade that destroyed his life. They would have to enter into the theatrical world that had been forced upon him by the accident, and that he now has chosen as the best alternative in coping with a shattered life. If this is madness, it is still more desirable than the alternative of what the world would consider his recovery.

Enrico's decision to seek refuge from the insanity of the life he would return to is determined both by his sensitivity to the shabby pity and remorse to which he would be subjected and by his natural sense of theater. Since he has been seen as an actor even when he did not intend to be one, and since it was a carefully prepared performance in a masked cavalcade that determined the nature of his madness, the choice to retain his persona as Enrico IV and structure the rest of his life around this figure is more understandable in him than it might be in others. The illusion of performance and the reality underneath had been confused in Enrico's wooing of Matilda and her mockery of his serious affection. His attempts to prove his intelligence after he realized that he was both spectator and performer merely furthered the illusion that he was a buffoon. The surface of his actions was taken as their only reality, with Matilda, Tito, and the others making no attempt to probe beyond the enigmatic personality he presented. Then the accident intervened and extinguished even more the separation between actor and his role, obliterating the "real" Enrico and substituting the historical personage of the masquerade. Enrico's decision to remain as the German king merely continued the performance he had been giving all his life. Now, however, he is consciously pretending to be both madman and historical character and exercising the control of director and playwright as well as actor.

Even though Enrico is a consummate actor, he does not have sufficient control over himself to keep the role from dominating the actor. Unlike the actress in *To Find Oneself,* who returns to the theater because she can find fulfillment only through her characterizations there, Enrico confuses artifice and reality and allows the two to merge. He lunges for Frida because she awakens in him his long dormant passion for Matilda, as well as the impossible dream of recapturing the past and his youth. With that action, however, he is drawn into real violence and traps himself in the role of Enrico IV for the rest of his life. He forgets the discipline of director-playwright he has been imposing on himself and his world and allows the impulses of the improvising actor to dictate his actions.

Enrico has only scorn for the real Matilda, both for her past behavior in mocking his expressions of love and for her present action of parading her current lover in front of him. Frida, on the other hand, represents the image that Enrico adored. His self-control, which has already been relaxed when he confided the truth of his pretense to his counselors, now deserts him as he tries to embrace Frida. When Tito acts to defend the young girl, he provides Enrico with an immediate obstacle to the gratification of his desires and an opportunity to gain revenge on the man who mocked him years ago, gained the affection of the woman he loved, and may even have caused the accident responsible for his madness. Whether Enrico's belief that his horse was pricked is paranoia or fact, and whether Tito was responsible or is believed responsible by Enrico, is left purposely ambiguous. The act of killing Tito, however, is something that had not been part of Enrico's conception of the role, and his "improvisation" here forces him to be trapped in that role permanently.

After Enrico stabs Tito, there is a brief but impassioned exchange. Matilda, the Doctor, and the others consider this act the proof that Enrico is truly mad. The dying Tito insists that Enrico is not mad.[10] The truth, as in much of Pirandello, lies in the middle. Enrico is both sane and insane at this moment. He has been overwhelmed by the phantasm of Matilda as a young woman. His emotions cause him to attempt a true act of madness, the recapturing of his youth. Of course he is a man who is grasping for a beautiful woman, but he is also a man near fifty wanting his love of many years ago. When Tito tries to protect Frida, he threatens Enrico's dream as well as the gratification of his passions. He also presents a tempting target for vengeance. Enrico acts to protect his "prize" and destroy his enemy. Yet because he acts in a purely emotional way, without any consideration of the consequences, he must now, as a result of his impulse, act the madman forever.

Previously Enrico had the freedom of dropping his persona of the German emperor whenever he wished. Now he will know that he is not the real Enrico, but will be unable to use this information. He will be locked into the character of Enrico, as he was when his madness was real. What began as the reality of madness and then became its illusion has now become a strange combination of both. His performance of madness, in Enrico's persona, must now become "real." Illusion and reality must become totally unified. Whether he is actually mad or sane is now unimportant, since his survival depends on his performance as Enrico IV. To remain free from punishment for his slaying of Tito, he must yield all possibility of gaining freedom from his mask. The actor has been permanently wedded to his role and cannot reveal to anyone the existence of a reality outside the artifice of his theatrical creation.

Pirandello's resolution of this play in ambiguity, in a netherworld between madness and sanity, theater and life, is not unexpected. It is consistent both with the ideas he has been expressing and with the way he has been presenting them. In fact, he has worked from the opening moment to create a sense of confusion, a dreamlike world of shadows where there is uncertainty as to time and place, what is real and what is not, and who is mad and who is sane.

The opening scene with the four counselors not only suggests the ambiguity of place and period discussed previously but creates the illusion of a certain kind of drama. *That's the Way Things Are* seems at first to be a mystery, but it is really something else. The theater plays appear at times to be either thesis plays or even melodramas, but they use only aspects of these genres. In *Enrico IV*, Pirandello begins with the illusion of a historical drama, long a dramatic staple, and then slowly reveals the reality underneath. The throne room can be in the Hartz castle, Worms, or Goslar. One of the counselors appears in a costume from another country and period. Other characters appear in modern dress. History is not the reality but an illusion that must be penetrated in order to discover what the play is really about. Even the title is misleading, suggesting Shakespeare's play of the same title when no connection exists.

Besides the ambiguity of time, place, and genre in the first scene, Pirandello indicates in his stage directions that it should be played rapidly. This is not because he is embarrassed by the exposition, as Eric Bentley argues,[11] but because he wants the play to first appear as a comedy, even a farce. The comic horseplay among the four counselors, with the mocking of the new man's confusion, is then interrupted by the arrival of Matilda and her party. Both Tito and the Doctor are fools; Tito plays the role consciously, while the Doctor does not. Although the outsiders have come for a serious purpose, they are still comic as well as sinister, like their counterpart chorus in *That's the Way Things Are*.

The tone shifts again with Enrico's arrival. He is ludicrous, but only superficially. The transition here is from comedy to something else. Both in the initial image of Enrico and in the way the play reveals him, there is the possibility of the movement from a comic surface to a more serious reality underneath. Since Enrico is the fulcrum of the play (although the play cannot succeed without strong performances of the supporting roles), it is through him that the transition through the various genres—or, perhaps more accurately, moods—is made.

Pirandello focuses his attention on the humoristic view of life, thus dramatizing a basically tragicomic vision. In this play he achieves that vision by running the gamut from comedy to tragedy. After the farcical beginnings, continuing through the comedy and then *umorismo* of the first two acts, he proceeds to the melodrama of Enrico's confrontation with the "living" paintings, his seizure of Frida, and murder of Tito in Act III. The full movement toward tragedy is completed with the final image, when Enrico gathers his counselors around him and tells them that they must now play their roles, together *per sempre:* forever. Enrico's freedom, his ability to deal with the insanity of his life and world through a mask of madness that could be shed at his discretion, has been destroyed by the very humanity, his passions of love and hate, that made him a performer before, during, and after his madness.

The freedom Enrico had exercised during his continuation of the role of the German monarch may have been largely illusory. The superiority he exercised in the knowledge of the true nature of his madness would be dissipated by its very use; once he revealed his mechanism of the masquerade as a refuge from life, he would no longer be able to continue isolating himself through its recourse. Yet the important thing was his belief in that freedom, whether real or illusory. At the final tableau Enrico realizes that he is trapped into his role once more, even though he has more awareness now than when he was condemned to his performance by the accident.

In *Feeling and Form,* Susanne Langer writes of the rhythms of comedy and tragedy and the forms encapsulating these rhythms.[12] In comedy the play's rhythm culminates in an open ending, while in tragedy the conclusion is closed. Although the total entrapment of his protagonist is not the only way in which Pirandello achieves the tragic, the denial of Enrico's freedom and his necessity of continuing a role he previously performed by choice is an important part of the completion of the arc from farce through comedy to tragicomedy, melodrama, and the final tragic image. Enrico is not dead, but he has no control over his life. The mask has become frozen to the face; the play has become real; and, most terrifying of all, it is a performance he must give "forever."

Much of the genius of this play lies in Pirandello's ability to tie its several strands together. The closed ending that ensnares Enrico in the tragedy of a life without alternatives gains its ultimate power from the summation of the theme of time that has been vital throughout. Enrico's loss of youth, its passing without his experiencing it, has been responsible both for the continuation of his mask of madness and, more important, for the action that now seals him in that role.

Even though the eight-hundred-year leap between the time of the masquerade and the present is an extensive time span, it is dwarfed by the period evoked in the play's final two words, *per sempre*. Enrico must play his part until his death, during a finite but at this point undetermined period, that for him is all the time he will have. It is forever. The twelve lost years that determined the shape of the rest of his life now pale before the indefinite time he faces as Enrico in the future, a future without hope and even the illusion of escape. Although the bleakness of that future combined with the barrenness of the past contribute to his tragedy, it is the forever with which Enrico ends the part of his life dramatized for an audience that ultimately defines the tragic nature of the play.

The tragic vision of *Enrico IV* is reinforced by Pirandello's customary technique of *umorismo*. The group of visitors attempt a totally intellectual analysis of Enrico, and instead of effecting a cure their intervention dooms him to a permanent acceptance of a reality that previously at least held the illusion of escape. The outsiders have not foreseen the possibility that Enrico IV might be a chosen role. They have not considered the effect that reawakening after the loss of a large segment of his life would have on a man like Enrico. They have always treated him as a freak, insensitive to the suffering that treatment generated. Their callousness pained him in the past; now it wreaks the ultimate havoc on his life and seals his fate forever.

The scientific jargon of the Doctor and the clumsily camouflaged curiosity of Enrico's family and friends establish their actions as being on the purely *avvertimento* level. Pirandello is not content, however, to prove the contrast between them and Enrico merely by the negative. Enrico's deep humanity and his concern with the *feelings* of others are sharply established in a brief but brilliant moment at the end of Act II. He has just revealed his recovery to the counselors, and now Giovanni, the old butler, is about to enter to help Enrico with his nightly routine. The young men want to mock Giovanni, making him play his role of monk even though it no longer holds meaning. Enrico is enraged by this suggestion. Why should the old man perform as a joke something he does out of love for Enrico? Only if the scene is played as if it were true will it have value. Ironically, the scene, which Giovanni plays for Enrico's benefit, will now be played for his own. Even if the old man is unaware that others are laughing at him, Enrico cannot bear to besmirch the purity of an act motivated by true kindness.

Enrico's reaction is essential to his character. He is not a pathological figure but a man who has been treated cruelly, both by his friends and by fate. He has sought refuge in a theatrical construct in order to deal with the insanity of his life in a fragmented world made even more chaotic by an enforced loss of twelve years. Enrico was an eccentric person even before the accident, yet his treatment of Giovanni illustrates a sense of compassion and sensitivity found nowhere else in the play. In the world of people like the Doctor and Matilda and Tito, it is madness to try to deal with life compassionately or to try to create a world of performance in order to express that kindness.

While *Enrico IV* is about madness, acting, aging, and time, it may most crucially be the tragedy of a man who tries to be a humorist, who tries to extend beyond the superficial level of the *avvertimento* to a *sentimento* level that combines thought and feeling in a response that may contradict the initial impression. As the conflict between Enrico and the others shows, the man who tries to use the *sentimento* approach instead of the *avvertimento* of the rest may be doomed to be an outcast, his sensitivity mockingly rejected. In order to survive in a world that rejects his compassionate vision, he is forced to become an actor, to play the role of another person. In an attempt to save his sanity he may have to play the madman, with the attendant risk that society will try to make his performance of that role a permanent one.

As both actor and madman, Enrico places himself in direct opposition to the society of which he is a part. He has never been normal in terms of the majority, but as the eccentric theatricalist of the crowd he could be tolerated, even enjoyed. Now, however, he is using the theater to exert a control over his life denied to everyone else. Even though he must maintain a theatrical illusion, he is free to perform in a world of his own choosing. Furthermore, if the others choose to interact with him, they must do so on his terms rather than on theirs.

Enrico's resolve to remain in a world of his own theatrical imagination isolates him from the influence of Matilda, Tito, and

Dr. Genoni (the man of science). He does not want their interference, their criticism, or their help. But in avoiding them, he is trying to play God. He wants to create his own universe and control his own destiny. Pirandello is suggesting that the only way this can be accomplished is through art. The playwright, director, designer, and actor are assuming godlike duties when they attempt to create something out of nothing, a world that did not exist previously and would not come into existence without them.

This artistic, and especially theatrical, impulse is vividly brought to life in Enrico. Yet the power and autonomy he seeks cannot be tolerated by the society as a whole. If that society cannot socialize him in the tradition of comedy, it will use the emotions and frailty of his humanity to trap him in tragic isolation, forcing him to choose between metaphoric imprisonment in a role and actual imprisonment for the crime they have instigated. Unlike *That's the Way Things Are,* where the humanity of the three victims triumphs over the chorus of busybodies, in this play Enrico's humanity, his need for love and his burning desire for his lost youth, are manipulated by the intellect-dominated outsiders into his destruction.

In viewing the conflict between Enrico and his society in this way, it is possible to extend the metaphor to Pirandello himself, as a logical extension of his Modernist self-referentiation. As an artist, Pirandello has tried to create a world, embody a vision, play God. Yet the majority of his audience has not been willing to accept what he has created, both because of the power it gives him and because of the judgments his world passes on theirs. The audience wants the artist to present a vision they can be comfortable with. If the artist dares to confront them with something else, they will fight with determination to make him change. If this fails, they at least try to force their interpretation on his work, either to make it more acceptable or to discredit or diminish its effectiveness.

Enrico IV is Pirandello's most satisfying play, not only because it embodies the theory of *umorismo* most completely, but also because it expresses that theory, and the accompanying ideas found throughout Pirandello's work, in totally theatrical terms. The originality of a self-conscious examination of the theater to establish its relationship to life has been surpassed in this play by the opposite mirror image. Life as theater is here explored with great depth and sophistication. In an individual's attempt to cope with insensitivity, the swift passage of time, and the branding of someone different as "madman," the theatricalization of life, with the consistent use of a role or mask placed between that individual and the world, may be necessary. Enrico has tried, with imagination and sympathy, to deal with the insanity and fragmentation of modern life. Pirandello's dramatization of how that attempt is twisted to become Enrico's entrapment rather than his refuge constitutes the ultimate genius, as well as the tragedy, of the play.

Conclusion

"I am the son of Chaos," Pirandello once wrote.[1] He was playing with words, since the small Sicilian town of his birth had the name of Caos. This Sicilian heritage is not difficult to locate in his work, even in those plays written after he abandoned the restrictions of Sicilian *verismo* and the dialect theater. His use of the themes of honor, jealousy, and revenge, as well as the sudden eruption of passion, all attest to the emotionality, the strictness of moral code, and the "operatic" nature that are sometimes associated with Italians in general and Sicilians in particular.

Yet Pirandello refers to much more than the geographical location of his birth, or even his ethnic background, when he identifies himself as "the son of Chaos." He was born three years before Italy achieved complete unification and nationhood. His parents were patriots who had fought for the Risorgimento, only to be cruelly disillusioned when Sicily was not treated equally by the other regions of the country. Although he was Italian, Pirandello was from the island part of the country that was and still is often looked down upon by the inhabitants of the "more cultured" north.

Pirandello's personal life also contributed to his sense of chaos. His adolescence was not marked by great instability, but his maturity was dominated by a marriage that brought great unhappiness. His wife was the choice of his father, who had arranged the match in order to consolidate two of the largest sulfur mines in the area. After an earthquake caused the failure of these mines, his wife began to lose her mind, her insanity taking the form of obsessive jealousy. She was positive that Pirandello was unfaithful to her, and nothing he could do or say could establish his innocence. When she finally accused him of having incestuous relations with their sixteen-year-old daughter, the young girl had to be sent away and Pirandello's attempts to care for his wife at home came to an end.[2]

The agonies of Pirandello's personal life were exacerbated by the politics and history of his time. When Italy entered World War I, his son, Stefano, was drafted and then captured by the Austrians. Pirandello corresponded with his son, not knowing if he would ever see him again. A few months before he completed his first great play, *That's the Way Things Are (If They Seem That Way to You)*, he wrote to Stefano, "I have read all the books of philosophy for your sake, and I will tell you what they said to me when you return. Very little, very little." [3]

Pirandello's personal suffering was emblematic of the crises being experienced by many others. The writings of Freud proclaiming the existence of the unconscious and the multiplicity of the personality suggested a general uncertainty that Pirandello had the misfortune to experience in more specific terms. The Great War that imprisoned his son was a tremendous shock that brought into question man's basic nature as a rational being. Human ingenuity was being harnessed for destruction instead of creation. The machine—glorified by many (such as the Futurists) as the symbol of progress and hope in the future—had been turned against man by other men. To Pirandello it was a symbol of alienation.

The war had been proof of the incoherence of human society as well as men's difficulty in communicating with each other. It was a form of chaos that was cataclysmic, both on the personal and the international levels. What was not needed was a drama that mirrored the chaos in a way that only reinforced it. Pirandello, as a man who had suffered deeply, had to communicate his sense of chaos, alienation, and fragmentation in such a way that his insights could be used to alleviate rather than contribute to the difficulties.

If Pirandello could not join the Futurists in their experiments designed to glorify mechanization and delineate the absurdity of bourgeois culture, neither could he accept the practices of realism used by that culture. "Reality" as it had been known was being shattered. Sigmund Freud, Albert Einstein, Friedrich Nietzsche, and others were positing significant new modes of perception. If a dramatist was not to be seen as a reactionary against these ideas, then not only must he incorporate some of them in his work but, more important, he must find a way to formulate them that would properly express their innovation. Pirandello needed a means of artistic expression that allowed him to explore the fragmentation and alienation of life as he saw and experienced it, while at the same time communicating the suffering caused by these conditions. The solution to his problem was, of course, *umorismo*.

Pirandello's use of *umorismo* allows him to suggest the intellectual quandary facing modern man: his difficulties in communication and perception, the multiplicity of his personality, and the breakdown of absolute values. At the same time, *umorismo* insures that it is the relationship these ideas bear to people, and not the ideas themselves, that takes precedence. Pirandello is willing to take the risk that he will be seen by some as an abstract or philosophical playwright; he is issuing a challenge. He is daring people to look at themselves and at life more deeply than they have done in the past. He is daring them to proceed beyond first impressions and superficial views, even if the insights gained by this more intense vision necessitate important changes both in one's opinion of a particular situation and one's mode of perception in general.

In the face of a reality that is no longer comprehensible and predictable, it is understandable that one might look to the mirror image of art in an attempt to give life order. Art is timeless, fixed, immutable. It supplies the constancy and security missing in an age of transition. Thus, life may try to adopt some of the practices of the theater in order to create stability. Yet if the theater is the true mirror of life, it must change at the same time that life does. If life is ambiguous, complex, and increasingly self-conscious and self-critical, then theater must be too. As life tries to borrow from the stability of art, then art is changing to become more like life. A reality that is firmly established can be reflected by realism; a reality that is in constant flux cannot.

As I have tried to suggest in my analysis of five of his greatest plays, the genius of Pirandello's accomplishment lies in his ability to suggest the need for the movement from an *avvertimento* to a *sentimento del contrario,* not merely in content, but in the dramatic encapsulation of those ideas. He became a theatrical innovator in a much deeper and more important sense than the Futurists, Surrealists, and Dadaists, whose alternative vision was couched in terms that made it inaccessible to those very people who needed to be confronted with it. Pirandello's initial reception gives evidence that his work also met resistance. Yet his retention of aspects of conventional realism allowed him both to draw his audience into his world in order to frustrate their old expectations and, more important, to communicate the relationship of his new vision to their everyday reality.

In a world dominated by alienation, fragmentation, and confusion, perhaps it takes a "son of Chaos" to show the way. Not only does Pirandello express the ideas and tenor of his age, but he does so in such a way as to suggest the new mode of perception necessary to survive in such a world. In a strange way he is a realist, not in the traditional sense, but in a new way that he defines. Reality for Pirandello is not drawing rooms, surface appearances, or the masks that others adopt. It is the suffering that lies underneath these concepts. Through *umorismo* we can gain an apprehension of that suffering. This *umorismo* is most effective when communicated in the theater, where, in the world of masks and illusions, we not only see our lives mirrored but hopefully also learn new ways of looking at and understanding it. The son of chaos does not bring order. He does bring an approach to the chaos that illuminates it and points the way to an intellectual and emotional understanding of the suffering that usually lies beneath.

Notes

All translations from the Italian, including *L'umorismo* and the plays, are by the author unless otherwise indicated. The matter quoted from Pirandello in Italian is taken from the Mondadori editions. Other terms and phrases are cited as they appear in the *Dizionario Scolastico,* edited by Nicola Spinelli (Torino: Società editrice internazionale, 1951).

Preface

1. Domenico Vittorini, *The Drama of Luigi Pirandello* (Philadelphia: University of Pennsylvania Press, 1935), p. vii. Pirandello wrote a letter to Vittorini because he recognized himself in Vittorini's analysis and was grateful for the appreciation of his work.
2. Robert Brustein, *The Theatre of Revolt* (Boston: Little, Brown, Atlantic Monthly Press, 1964), p. 283
3. Brustein, *The Theatre of Revolt,* p. 283. Walter Starkie, in his book, *Luigi Pirandello (1867–1936)* (Berkeley and Los Angeles: University of California Press, 1967), is especially sharp in his attack on Pirandello as a nihilistic writer. Gaspar Giudice, one of the most perceptive contemporary Italian critics, sees several of Pirandello's major

plays as his vengeance on life, with *Così è (se vi pare) (That's the Way Things Are–If They Seem That Way to You)* based on the annihilation of all values. See his *Pirandello* (Torino: Unione Tipografico Editrice Torinese, 1963), p. 318.
4. *Almanaco letterario Mondadori* (1927), quoted in Giudice, *Pirandello*, p. 388.
5. Anne Righter, in *Shakespeare and the Idea of the Play* (London: Chatto and Windus, 1962), discusses the self-conscious use of the stage in Shakespeare's work. Lionel Abel goes even further in *Metatheatre*, proposing the separate genre of metatheater for those works where "the playwright has the obligation to acknowledge in the very structure of his play that it was his imagination which controlled the event from beginning to end" (New York: Hill & Wang, 1963), p. 61. Beside Shakespeare, Abel names Racine, Molière, and Calderón as early practitioners of metatheatre. Playwrights are not the only writers to present such a vision. Cervantes not only has Don Quixote compare stage roles to roles assumed in life, with death as the great equalizer, but allows Sancho to reply, "It is a fine comparison, though not so new but that I have heard it many times before" *(Don Quixote,* trans. Samuel Putnam [London, 1953], Part II, Book iii, 12).
6. Even just on the level of content, of course, Pirandello's juxtaposition of life and theater becomes much more complex than the simple equation of the different phases of life with theatrical roles.

Chapter 1

1. Pirandello, *L'umorismo,* in *Saggi, Poesie, Scritti varii,* Manlio Lo Vecchio Musti (Milan: Arnoldo Mondadori Editore, 1965). For an English translation of *L'umorismo,* see *On Humor,* introduced, translated and annotated by Antonio Illiano and Daniel P. Testa. (Chapel Hill, North Carolina: University of North Carolina Press). An essay, "On Pirandello's Humorism," by Dante Della Terza can be found in *Veins of Humor,* edited by Harry Levin. (Cambridge, Massachusetts: Harvard University Press, 1972).
2. Adriano Tilgher, *Voci del Tèmpo* (1921) and *Studi sul teatro contemporàneo* (1923) Rome: Libreria di scienze e lettere.
3. Gaspar Giudice, *Pirandello* (Torino: Unione Tipografico Editrice Torinese, 1963), pp. 389–400. Giudice's book has replaced Nardelli's *L'uomo segreto* (Milan: Mondadori, 1944), a biography written by one of Pirandello's friends with his assistance, as the standard biographical-critical analysis of his life. The English translation published by the Oxford Press is an abridgment of the original work.
4. Ibid., p. 394.
5. "Directing Pirandello Today," an interview with Gino Rizzo, *Tulane*

Drama Review 10, no. 3 (Spring 1966). This issue of *TDR* published several articles on Pirandello and a translation of an excerpt from *L'umorismo*.
6. Ibid., p. 79.
7. Starkie has translated this passage from Tilgher, who cites it in *Voci del Tempo*. Pirandello is certainly not alone in his fascination with the mirror image. Jean Cocteau, for example, identified the reflective image as a particularly suggestive and appropriate one both in his writings and such films as *Orpheus* and *The Beauty and the Beast*.
8. I have chosen to use this translation for the title *Così è (se vi pare)* because I find the two English versions commonly used to be unsatisfactory. Eric Bentley's *Right You Are (If You Think You Are)* connotes an aggressive subjectivity lacking in the original, while Arthur Livingston's *It is So (If You Think So)*, in Bentley's edition of *Naked Masks* (New York: Dutton, 1952), also misses the idea of seeming suggested by *pare*. *Così è* literally translates as "Thus it is," but I have chosen a more idiomatic and smoother alternative.
9. Eric Bentley entitles his collection of five Pirandello plays *Naked Masks*, but Pirandello uses the title to refer to his entire canon of dramatic work.
10. Walter Starkie writes that some critics refer to *Enrico IV* as "the Hamlet of the twentieth century" and identifies both protagonists as humorists. *(Luigi Pirandello 1867–1936* [Berkeley and Los Angeles: University of California Press, 1967], p. 189.) Eric Bentley, in an essay *"Enrico IV,"* in *Theatre of War* (New York: Viking Press, 1972), also sees the play as Pirandello's *Hamlet*, identifying Belcredi as its Claudius, Matilda its Gertrude, and Frida its Ophelia. He then adds; "And Hamlet's antic disposition has spread itself over the whole life of the Pirandellian protagonist" (p. 38). Anne Paolucci continues the exploration of this relationship in *Pirandello's Theatre: The Recovery of the Modern Stage for Dramatic Art* (Carbondale and Edwardsville: Southern Illinois University Press, 1974).
11. Gregory Battcock, ed., *The New Art* (New York: Dutton, 1973), pp. 66–77.
12. Ibid., p. 67.
13. Pirandello, *L'umorismo*, p. 146.

Chapter 2

1. Robert Brustein, *The Theatre of Revolt* (Boston: Little, Brown, Atlantic Monthly Press, 1964), p. 284. D'Annunzio's work was particularly anathema to Pirandello, both because of its extreme emphasis on the sound and not the sense of language and because Eleanora Duse, Italy's leading actress, enacted most of D'Annunzio's heroines and never appeared in one of his plays.

2. Appendix to Eric Bentley's translation of *Right You Are (If You Think You Are)* (New York: Columbia University Press, 1954), p. 133.
3. The turbulence of World War I also contributed to Pirandello's dissatisfaction with tradition and time-honored practices. His son, Stefano, was captured by the Austrians, adding personal involvement to the social and political analysis he would have given to the situation.
4. For an English translation of the story, see Bentley's translation of *Right You Are,* cited in note 5.
5. Gaspar Giudice, *Pirandello* (Torino: Unione Tipografico Editrice Torinese, 1963), p. 319.
6. The short story on which the play is based does not contain the character of Laudisi, nor anyone who performs his function. The townspeople are also not given individual names or characterizations but are referred to merely as the group of people to whom the Ponza-Frola family is held accountable.
7. Eric Bentley, *"Right You Are,"* in *Theatre of War* (New York: Viking Press, 1972), p. 25. For the ideas of the Italian director Giorgio DiLullo, whose production of *Così è* was first produced in Rome in the spring of 1972, see "Il coro sei tu" in *Il Dramma* (April 1972): ("The Chorus Is You") 82-85.
8. Giudice, *Pirandello,* p. 319.
9. Lionel Abel thus could not be more incorrect when he states that "In fact, the Italian dramatist is lacking in moral interest: his dramaturgy counts only when he is excited by the metaphysical side of a conflict" *(Metatheatre)* (New York: Hill & Wang, 1963), p. 111.
10. Their suffering has its source, not in the dilemma which they face among themselves, but in the personal tragedy they have recently experienced. Their village has just been destroyed by an earthquake, killing many relatives and friends. Although the earthquake has also destroyed any records that might establish the authenticity of one story over another, it is the suffering that has forced them to seek a new life that is Pirandello's primary concern.
11. Richard Gilman, in *The Making of Modern Drama* (New York: Farrar, Straus & Giroux, 1974), identifies Laudisi as "a raisonneur-like character who clearly stands in for Pirandello" (p. 169). Brustein identifies him as an *Eiron* whose function is to whip the chorus with his savage laughter. Although Brustein does identify Pirandello's frustration of the chorus as more important to the play than the "philosophy," he fails to include Laudisi as one of the characters whose vision is shown to be limited *(The Theatre of Revolt,* pp. 294-295.) Bentley claims that Laudisi is "Harlequin in modern dress, a Harlequin who has invaded the realm of philosophy and who behaves there as he behaved everywhere else" *("Right You Are,"* in *Theatre of War,* p. 26). Although Laudisi may make fun of everything, as Bentley suggests, Pirandello criticizes this attitude in a way that Bentley ignores. Anne

Paolucci recognizes the ambiguity in Pirandello's treatment of Laudisi when she says, "His very scepticism is a sign of his inability to recognize truth" *(Pirandello's Theatre: The Recovery of the Modern Stage for Dramatic Art* [Carbondale and Edwardsville: Southern Illinois University Press, 1974], p. 86), and she is one of the very few to do so. From the opposite direction comes Jan Moestrup's suggestion that "it is unwise to place too much emphasis on the figure of Laudisi in a production of the play. It is a mistake to emphasize his function as a theorist and the conceptual aspect of the play. This is the only time a theorist appears in one of Pirandello's great plays, and he is actually a survivor from among the narrators of the short stores," *(The Structural Patterns of Pirandello's Work* [Odense: Odense University Press, 1972], p. 154).

12. Robert S. Dombrowski in his article, "Laudisi's Laughter and the Social Dimension of *'Right You Are (If You Think You Are),'* " *Modern Drama* 16 (1973): 337–346, sees the entire play as an elaborate joke, with Laudisi's laughter "a spontaneous show of approval for a humorous situation" (p. 342), "the effect of an exhilarating sense of being liberated from conventional thought patterns" (p. 344).
13. Giudice, *Pirandello,* p. 57.
14. Ibid., p. 247.

Chapter 3

1. Robert Brustein, *The Theatre of Revolt* (Boston: Little, Brown, Atlantic Monthly Press, 1964), p. 304.
2. In Italian the word for a theater audience and the public is the same, *il pubblico,* while the word *l'udienza* is reserved for an audience in the sense of a meeting with an official such as the pope or a president.
3. In *Modern Drama from Ibsen to Brecht* (Oxford: Oxford University Press, 1968), Raymond Williams discusses Brecht's main artistic goal as the presentation of a "complex way of seeing," a concept Brecht himself uses in his theoretical writings.
4. Domenico Vittorini, *The Drama of Luigi Pirandello* (Philadelphia: University of Pennsylvania Press, 1935), p. 228.
5. The composition of the three plays covers almost the entire decade of the 1920s. *Six Characters in Search of an Author* appeared in 1921; *Each in His Own Way* in 1924, two years after *Enrico IV;* while *Tonight We Improvise,* written in 1929, is among Pirandello's last works.
6. Giudice recounts the opening night of *Six Characters* where the audience came near to rioting and Pirandello had to seek refuge in a taxi because of the virulence of the crowd's reaction after the performance. *(Pirandello* [Torino: Unione Tipografico Editrice Torinese, 1963], pp. 368–370.)
7. Pirandello's advocacy of real masks is rarely followed in production,

162   *Dreams of Passion*

        since stylized makeup and lighting can suggest the same type of separation without imposing a barrier that might rob the characters of some of their humanity.
8. Giudice, *Pirandello*, p. 338.
9. Ibid., pp. 408–409.
10. Ibid., p. 337.
11. Richard Gilman, *The Making of Modern Drama* (New York: Farrar, Straus & Giroux, 1974), p. 179.
12. The most widely known English translation, done by Arthur Livingston and found in Bentley's edition of *Naked Masks,* is based on the first version and thus ends without the final image.
13. In *The Idea of a Theatre* Francis Fergusson identifies the Aristotelian action of *Six Characters* as "to take the stage" (Garden City, New York: Doubleday Anchor Books, 1952, p. 204).
14. Giudice, *Pirandello*, p. 248.
15. Ibid., p. 298.

Chapter 4

1. Gaspar Giudice, *Pirandello* (Torino: Unione Tipografico Editrice Torinese, 1963), pp. 368–370.
2. The French term *roman à clef* refers to this phenomenon in the novel.
3. Eric Bentley, ed., *Naked Masks* (New York: Dutton, 1952). Livingston includes only the program note (see the end of the quotation) and a sentence asking the audiece to remain seated for the choral interludes.
4. The staging of this "event" as the prologue to his play illustrates Pirandello's interest in extending the boundaries of the theater. This prologue has some of the flavor of the "Happening" or the Futurist, Surrealist, and Dadaist experiments that preceded it. Yet at the same time the free form does not exist for its own sake but as a means of preparing the audience for what they will encounter inside the theater.
5. For further discussion of the mirror gone crazy in *Each in His Own Way,* see Anne Paolucci's *Pirandello's Theatre: The Recovery of the Modern Stage for Dramatic Art* (Carbondale and Edwardsville: Southern Illinois University Press, 1974), pp. 53–58.
6. Luigi Squarzina, "Notes for 'Each in His Own Way,'" *Tulane Drama Review* 10, no. 3 (Spring 1966) 87–90.
7. As Oscar Wilde writes in *De Profundis,* "the supreme vice is shallowness."

Chapter 5

1. See J. L. Styan's *The Dark Comedy* (London: Cambridge University Press, 1962) for a discussion of this phenomenon.
2. Robert Brustein, *The Theatre of Revolt* (Boston: Little, Brown, Atlantic Monthly Press, 1964), p. 305.
3. Even though Hinkfuss's appearance may undercut his ideas, the opposite effect is also achieved: his articulateness and determination, even if somewhat misguided, make the audience less aware of his physical strangeness. This of course parallels the progression of the humorist's perception of the old woman of *L'umorismo*.
4. Just as the lack of structure and discipline in Italian life, appealing though it may be, often leads dangerously close to chaos.
5. Domenico Vittorini, *The Drama of Luigi Pirandello* (Philadelphia: University of Pennsylvania Press, 1935), p. 305.
6. This reference to cuckolding brings in another basic icon of Italian culture. The most common symbol for a foolish man in Italy is the cuckold, both in a literary tradition extending back to Boccaccio and commedia dell'arte and in contemporary practice. The extension of two fingers to designate the cuckold's horns is a common sign of contempt and mockery even today.
7. In his production of *Tonight We Improvise* at the Teatro Stábile di Genova in the spring of 1972, Squarzina staged the intermezzo scenes in various parts of the theater auditorium, with a spotlight drawing the seated audience's attention to each succeeding scene. While this staging allowed everyone to experience the complete text, it did eliminate some of Pirandello's complexity and experimentation.
8. Federico Fellini captures the same sense of *umorismo* in his film *The Clowns*, when he presents the funeral of a clown as simultaneously comic and sad.
9. Pirandello was well qualified to write of this contrast. Born and raised in Sicily, the most southern extremity of Italy and a location known for tempestuous passions, he studied philology, a discipline of strict rules and order, in Bonn, where he encountered the more ordered Germanic approach to life. Thereafter he returned to Rome where he lived and made his career, perhaps trying to reconcile the two conflicting milieus and life-styles he had witnessed.
10. Brustein, *The Theatre of Revolt*, p. 308.

Chapter 6

1. For a discussion of the effect the insanity of Pirandello's wife had on his life and work, see Gaspar Giudice's *Pirandello* (Torino: Unione Tipografico Editrice Torinese, 1963).

2. Robert Brustein, *The Theatre of Revolt* (Boston: Little, Brown, Atlantic Monthly Press, 1964), pp. 296–298.
3. I am speaking here from the point of view of the visitors, who of course do not know that Enrico is cured. Pirandello's point is that, despite their intentions, their actions are indefensible.
4. Enrico refers to Matilda as "Madonna," which is translated in the Storer translation in Bentley's *Naked Masks* as "Madam" (New York: Dutton, 1952). The Italian term has religious connotations suggesting Mary, the mother of Christ, and can imply Enrico's still existent affection for Matilda, even as he tries to remove the "mask" of makeup from her face. "Madonna" can also have an ironic connotation, since he later expresses contempt for her by calling her a whore.
5. Brustein, *The Theatre of Revolt*, p. 299. Brustein, however, takes Enrico's attempt at recapturing his youth, his "masquerade within a masquerade," seriously, without mentioning the ironic twist Enrico supplies in his interchange with Matilda.
6. Giudice, *Pirandello*, p. 172.
7. Ibid., pp. 300–301.
8. Ibid., p. 335.
9. Of course some of the same questions about acting and madness can be asked of Hamlet as well.
10. This argument echoes the cries of "pretense" and "reality" that greet the death of the little boy in *Six Characters*. In that case as well, there is some degree of truth in the claims made by both sides.
11. Eric Bentley, *"Enrico IV,"* in *Theatre of War* (New York: Viking Press, 1972), p. 33.
12. Susanne K. Langer, *Feeling and Form* (New York: Scribner's, 1953), pp. 326–269.

Chapter 7

1. Gaspar Giudice, *Pirandello* (Torino: Unione Tipografico Editrice Torinese, 1963), p. 15.
2. Ibid., pp. 297–303.
3. Ibid., p. 317.

Index

Abel, Lionel, 158, 160
As Before, Better Than Before (Come prima, meglio di prima), 50
Avvertimento del contrario (awareness of the opposite), 2, 3, 14, 27, 41, 42, 59, 64, 70, 91, 92, 93, 120, 121, 129, 133, 139, 149, 150

Balanchine, George, 17
Battcock, Gregory, 159
Beckett, Samuel, 17
Bentley, Eric, 23, 24, 147, 159, 160, 162, 163
Bergson, Henri, 5
Berlin, 99
Boccaccio, 163
Brecht, Bertolt, 17, 112, 161
Brook, Peter, 17
Brustein, Robert, vii, viii, 47-48, 102, 122-23, 125, 135, 157, 159, 160, 161, 163-64
Building a Character, 14

Calderón, 158
Cecè, 23

Cervantes, 158
Cocteau, Jean, 159
Commedia a chiave (Play With A Key), 76, 79, 82, 85, 86, 92, 94, 101, 123, 162
Commedia dell'arte, 12, 13, 50, 85, 99
Costruirsi (to build oneself up), 12, 14, 15, 17
Cubism, 16, 49

Dadaism, 22, 156, 162
D'Annunzio, Gabriele, 22, 68, 159
Della Terza, Dante, 158
De Profundis, 162
Diana and the Tuda (Diana e la tuda), 6
DiLullo, Giorgio, 24, 160
Dizionario Scolastico, 157
Dombrowski, Robert, 161
Don Quixote, 158
Duse, Eleanora, 159

Each in His Own Way (Ciascuno a suo modo), 7, 8, 49, 50, 72, 74-95, 96, 98, 106, 122, 123, 161-62
Einstein, Albert, 155
Élan vital, 5

166 INDEX

Enrico IV (Henry IV), 1, 15, 91, 99, 124-56, 159, 163-64

Feeling and Form, 148, 164
Fellini, Federico, 163
Freud, Sigmund, 5, 154, 155
Futurism, 22, 49, 68, 123, 154, 155, 156, 162

Genet, Jean, 17
German-Italian dichotomy, 122, 163
Gilman, Richard, 68, 160, 162
Giudice, Gaspar, 6, 82, 122, 157, 158, 160, 161, 162, 163, 164
Greenberg, Clement, 16-17, 25, 159

Hamlet, xv, 15-16, 159, 164
Hegel, Georg W.F., 5

Illiano, Antonio, 158
Il Trovatore, 117-119
Ionesco, Eugène, 17
Italian life and culture, 50, 98-99, 101, 107-08, 117, 153, 163

Joyce, James, 49

Kant, Immanuel, 17

Langer, Susanne, 148, 164
Levin, Harry, 158
Liolà, 23, 50
Livingston, Arthur, 76, 91, 162
L'umorismo (On Humor), ix-x, 1-21, 27, 33, 35, 64, 82, 86, 91, 105, 121, 130, 131, 133, 158, 159, 163

Makeup, 2-3, 47, 130-33
Martinetti, Filippo Tomaso, 68
Maschere nude (Naked Masks), 12, 159
Masks, 12, 14, 19, 55, 113, 161-62
Modernism, 16-17, 21, 25, 94, 97, 151
Moestrup, Jan, 161
Molière, 158
Mortier, Alfred, 67

Nardelli, Federico, 158
Natoli, Luigi, 66
Nietzsche, Friedrich, 5, 155
Nobel Prize, vii

Orpheus, 159

Paolucci, Anne, 159, 160-61, 162
Paris, 74
Pirandello (Gaspar Giudice), 6, 82, 122, 157, 158, 160, 161, 162, 163, 164
Pirandello, Antonietta, 40-41, 72, 137-38, 154
Pirandello, Lietta, 37, 72, 154
Pirandello, Stefano, 154
Pitoëff, Georges, 74
Proust, Marcel, 49
Purgatory, 48

Racine, Jean, 158
Raisonneur, vii, 35, 46, 82, 102, 160
Reinhardt, Max, 102
Righter, Anne, 158
Ring cycle, 131
Risorgimento, 153
Rizzo, Gino, 158

Satire, 18
Sentimento del contrario (feeling of the opposite), 2, 3, 11, 14, 20, 27-28, 41, 42, 43, 58-59, 64, 92, 93, 112, 115, 120, 129, 133, 142, 150, 156
Shakespeare, William, ix, xv, 15-16, 158, 159, 164
Shaw, George Bernard, 5
Sicily, 22, 23, 97-98, 101, 104, 153
"Signora Frola and Signor Ponza, Her Son-in-law," 23, 160
Six Characters in Search of an Author (Sei personaggi in cerca d'autore), 1, 6, 12, 17, 20, 25, 47-73, 74, 75, 76, 85, 89, 91, 94, 96, 102, 122, 123, 124, 138, 161
Spinelli, Nicola, 157
Squarzina, Luigi, 7-8, 85, 158, 162, 163
Stanislavski, Konstantin, 14

Starkie, Walter, 157, 159
Studi sul teatro contemporaneo, 6
Styan, J.L., 163
Surrealism, 22, 156, 162
Svevo, Italo, 49

Teatro d'arte di Roma, 103
Teatro dello specchio (theater of the mirror), 8, 12, 15, 39-41, 67, 75-76, 84, 86-87, 115-16, 120
Teatro Stábile di Genova, 163
Teatro Stábile di Roma, 7
Testa, Daniel, 158
That's the Way Things Are—If They Seem That Way to You (Cosí èse vi pare), 9, 12, 22-46, 49, 50, 52, 53, 54, 67, 83, 91, 100, 147, 151, 154, 160, 161, 169
Theater trilogy, x, 51, 52, 74-75, 85, 96, 97, 120, 122, 123, 124, 133, 161
The Beauty and the Beast, 159
The Jar (La giara), 23, 50
The Rules of the Game (Il giuoco delle parti), 55, 69
The Theater of Revolt, vii, viii, 47-48, 102, 122-23, 125, 135, 157, 159, 160, 161, 163-64
"The Tragedy of a Character," 66
Tilgher, Adriano, 5-7, 82, 122, 159, 165
To Clothe the Naked (Vestire gli ignudi), 75

To Find Oneself (Trovarsi), 13-14, 145
Tonight We Improvise (Questa sera si recita a soggeto), 50, 74, 75, 85, 89, 91, 96-123, 130, 138, 161
Tragicomedy, 100, 147

Umorismo, 1-21, 26, 46, 49, 50, 70, 73, 92, 93, 94, 100, 101, 105, 109, 112-13, 118, 121, 131, 147, 149, 151, 155, 156, 163

Valkyrie, 131
Verdi Giuseppe, 117-19
Verga, Giovanni, 23
Verismo, 22, 25, 67, 153
Vittorini, Domenico, vii, 84, 157, 161, 163
Voci del tèmpo, 5

Wagner, Richard, 131
When Someone is Somebody (Quando si e qualcuno), 6
Wilde, Oscar, 162
Williams, Raymond, 161
Woolf, Virginia, 49
World War I, 154, 160

Yeats, William Butler, 48